THE SECRETS OF TAE KWON DO

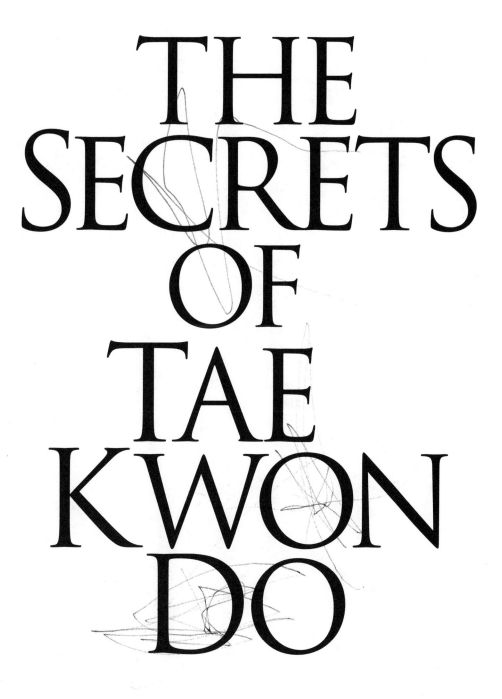

THE SECRETS OF TAE KWON DO

Principles and Techniques for Beginners

JENNIFER LAWLER

MASTERS PRESS

NTC/Contemporary Publishing Group

Library of Congress Cataloging-in-Publication Data

Lawler, Jennifer, 1965–.
    The secrets of tae kwon do / by Jennifer Lawler.
       p.   cm.
    ISBN 1-57028-202-1
    1. Tae kwon do.   I. Title.
GV1114.9.L38   1998
796.815′3—dc21   98-31340
                                   CIP

Cover design by Nick Panos
Cover photograph by Jennifer Lawler
Interior design by Kim Heusel
Interior photographs by Jennifer Lawler

Published by Masters Press
A division of NTC/Contemporary Publishing Group, Inc.
4255 West Touhy Avenue, Lincolnwood (Chicago), Illinois 60712-1975 U.S.A.
Copyright © 1999 by Jennifer Lawler
Printed in the United States of America
International Standard Book Number: 1-57028-202-1

99 00 01 02 03 04 VL 20 19 18 17 16 15 14 13 12 11 10 9 8 7 6 5 4 3 2

Contents

Acknowledgments

Although my development as a martial artist has been aided and influenced by countless people, I must thank my instructors, Masters Don and Susan Booth, for their kindness and patience over the past half-dozen years; Master Jung of Cedar Rapids, Iowa, for sharing his vision of a world in which everyone practices Tae Kwon Do and is therefore at peace; and all of the black belts at New Horizons Black Belt Academy of Tae Kwon Do for their support, encouragement and loyalty throughout a long and sometimes difficult journey.

Special appreciation goes to the martial artists who patiently posed while I took photos. My sincerest thanks to Carol Stambaugh Frailey; Vicky Anderson, Brian "Chip" Anderson and Chantal Anderson; J. P. Merz; Chad Wehr; Lou Ann Lee; Margaret Cardinal; Joanne Cox; and Dave Buller. Without all of you I would be one desperate writer.

Also, the role my husband, Bret Kay, played must be acknowledged. Not only was his technical advice welcome, but without his patience, forbearance and sense of humor, none of my books would be in print. He is the martial artist I can only strive to become.

And finally, to my delightful Buddha baby Jessica, for showing me the real meaning of indomitable spirit. It is truly remarkable that the heart of a lion can reside in the smallest one among us.

THE
SECRETS
OF
TAE
KWON
DO

Part I

1

Introduction to Tae Kwon Do

What Is Tae Kwon Do?

Originating in Korea, Tae Kwon Do is a modern martial art that is based on ancient methods of combat. Like all martial arts, it is a system of practical techniques used for fighting in almost any possible situation. But Tae Kwon Do is much more than just an efficient system for fending off attackers. It is also a way of life. By practicing Tae Kwon Do and its related ethics, a student will become a better person, not just a better fighter. It is through the balance of mental, emotional, physical and spiritual elements that true growth as a martial artist occurs.

The Meaning of Tae Kwon Do

Tae Kwon Do was once known as "Korean Karate" in the United States, because people were familiar with the Japanese art of Karate but few had ever heard of Tae Kwon Do. Like Karate, Tae Kwon Do emphasizes powerful punches and explosive attacks. Tae Kwon Do, however, also emphasizes high kicks, jumping kicks and flying kicks that are spectacular and showy. Thus it earned its name, which translates as "the art of hand and foot fighting."

Tae Kwon Do is an empty-hand martial art, meaning that it doesn't teach the use of weapons, although it teaches how to defend against weapons. Like most martial arts, it emphasizes defensive fighting. The goal is not to harm others or to instigate attacks, but simply to keep from being harmed yourself. Self-defense, therefore, is taught on three levels: escape, control and counter. A Tae Kwon Do practitioner always begins with an escaping technique and only when further attacked or confronted will escalate to the more violent levels of self-defense.

Essential Elements of Tae Kwon Do

In addition to the kicks and punches that resemble Karate, Tae Kwon Do also favors takedown techniques and throws, such as are found in Aikido and Judo. Other essential elements in the arsenal of Tae Kwon Do techniques include joint locks and vital point strikes, which more skilled practitioners are able to use in their fighting. Tae Kwon Do is further characterized by its emphasis on board breaking, which makes it different from other systems of martial arts. Board breaking is used to demonstrate power, technique and mental discipline. Stu-

3

Tae Kwon Do incorporates controlling and trapping techniques, above, as well as joint locks (left).

dents of all ranks are expected to perform board breaks when called upon to do so, with advanced students performing more difficult breaks.

Mental and Emotional Aspects

But Tae Kwon Do doesn't rely only on physical techniques. It stresses that only through the correct balance of body, mind and nature can true martial arts achievements be reached. In this way, Tae Kwon Do is more than simply a method of self-defense. It is also a way of approaching life and learning to live harmoniously. For this reason, anyone interested in pursuing Tae Kwon Do must also be committed to following its ethics, called the

Five Tenets, which are discussed in Chapter 4. Practitioners must also be open to experiences that build character, require self-discipline and promote balance and moderation in all things.

Physical Aspects

Although the mental and emotional aspects of Tae Kwon Do will be explained, this book will focus on teaching the physical techniques of Tae Kwon Do because it is through the continual practice of these techniques that the mastery of all areas of Tae Kwon Do is achieved.

The physical practice of Tae Kwon Do is generally broken into four stages: fighting techniques, forms, sparring and self-defense. Each of these areas is essential and all are interrelated. That is, they depend upon one another. To improve your martial arts skills, you must spend equal amounts of practice time in each of the four areas. To practice sparring but not forms makes you a martial artist who lacks balance, and therefore you may miss opportunities for personal growth and martial arts success.

Fighting Techniques

Fighting techniques are the building blocks of Tae Kwon Do. Therefore, they are the first thing you learn. Punches, kicks, blocks and stances must be individually learned and understood before they can be incorporated into forms, sparring or self-defense. The basic techniques can be learned very quickly, but will take years to perfect. This easy-to-learn, hard-to-master element is the challenge and the delight of Tae Kwon Do. Nonetheless, with serious practice, competence can be acquired in just a few months. This means that although your side kick won't be perfect, you'll still be able to stop an attacker with it.

Ten Basic Movements

Ten basic movements make up the core techniques of Tae Kwon Do. They are the techniques upon which all others build. Students are expected to memorize and perform the ten basic movements before they progress beyond the white belt ranking. The movements are performed in the following order:

1. Low Block
2. Middle Punch (straight punch to the middle section)
3. High Punch (straight punch to the high section)
4. High Block
5. Middle Front Kick, Punch (front kick followed immediately by a straight punch, both to the middle section)
6. High Front Kick, Punch (front kick followed immediately by a straight punch, both to the high section)
7. Inside-Outside Crescent Block
8. Outside-Inside Crescent Block
9. Double Knife Hand Block
10. Two-Finger Strike

(Some schools substitute a single knife hand block for number 9 and a knife hand strike for number 10.)

Board Breaking

As Tae Kwon Do students master the fighting techniques, they are expected to demonstrate their newly acquired skills through the practice of board breaking. Using techniques they have learned, Tae Kwon Do students attempt to break one-inch-thick pine boards. Black belts sometimes break concrete blocks. The purpose of board and block breaking is to develop focus and self-confidence. If a technique is executed correctly, the board will break. But because it can seem difficult or impossible, the idea of board breaking can be very intimidating.

For this reason, board breaking requires mental mastery as well. To attempt to break a board even though you are intimidated is the kind of experience that allows Tae Kwon Do practitioners to face an attacker even if they're afraid. The idea isn't that you'll never be afraid (fear is sometimes a perfectly logical response to a given situation), but that you'll learn to fight in spite of your fear and you'll learn to overcome your fear. This extends far beyond the fear of physical danger, and includes other fears that keep people from making the most of their lives.

Board breaking without the professional supervision of a qualified black belt is strongly discouraged.

Forms

Once the basic fighting techniques are acquired, the Tae Kwon Do practitioner puts these together to practice forms, sparring and self-defense. After learning a few techniques, a Tae Kwon Do student is taught a beginner form. *Chon-ji* is the first form a student learns. A form is simply a set pattern of techniques that a martial artist memorizes and practices. This allows the martial artist to work on techniques in a series and to combine techniques together. A form is also a good way to practice a wide variety of techniques in a small amount of space. Forms are considered the "art" in martial art, emphasizing balance, grace and timing. In Tae Kwon Do, the ability to practice a form with power, agility and beauty is considered essential to the development of all skills.

In addition to the improvement of physical skills, forms are essential for the cultivation of an empty mind. An empty mind is one that filters out all distractions and doesn't think but simply reacts appropriately. Tae Kwon Do practitioners are often told they "think too much," especially at the beginning of their training. The idea is that instead of analyzing, processing and considering what to do, the martial artists should just do the form (or the fighting technique, or the sparring match). Thinking too much slows us down, impairs our reflexes and allows mental doubt, indecision and confusion to creep in. Therefore, forms are memorized until no thought is needed to perform the techniques correctly. This helps to develop an empty mind.

As the martial artist develops, forms become more difficult to perform and master. Depending on the style of Tae Kwon Do, a student may learn one, two or more forms per belt level (also called "rank"). All forms must be memorized so that they can be performed or taught to another student at any time. That is, every form, even the beginner form that white belts learn (*Chon-ji*), must be memorized and practiced even by black belts, who might be called upon to teach it at any time. Advanced black belts create their own forms and name them as part of their promotion tests.

Freestyle Sparring

Freestyle sparring is the next element in training. Once a student has learned basic techniques and how they can be put together, he or she is ready for sparring. In sparring, partners attack and defend as if they were in an actual confrontation, but of course under carefully controlled circumstances. Fighters wear safety gear, restrict techniques to certain target areas and cannot use especially dangerous techniques. Although a partner is necessary to learn to spar competitively, practitioners without partners can learn many of the necessary skills by shadow sparring and by sparring a heavy bag.

Self-Defense

Self-defense practice is the final component of the study of Tae Kwon Do. Self-defense requires a knowledge of the basic techniques, which it builds on through the practice of realistic scenarios, such as an attacker grabbing you by the arm or the sleeve. The idea is to make responses to common attacks almost automatic. This ensures that Tae Kwon Do practitioners don't freeze when confronted. In addition to kicks and punches, self-defense techniques include joint locking and vital point striking.

Ranking System

When taking formal Tae Kwon Do classes, you will be expected to improve with time and training. These improvements in skill level are assigned a rank. Ranks are indicated by belt color. Tae Kwon Do starts, as do most martial arts, with a white belt. This is the beginner who has little or no knowledge of Tae Kwon Do. The colored belts include yellow, orange, green, blue, purple, brown and red. Not all schools use all the colors (some of the colors are interchangeable), but most schools proceed in this order of colors. Ranks are sometimes subdivided further; for instance, a green belt might have two levels, low and high. The "high" green belt would indicate a greater level of competence. Colored belt ranks are called *gup*.

Meaning of Colored Belts

Each belt color symbolizes a stage of growth in the process of Tae Kwon Do training. White belt, the beginner level, symbolizes innocence and lack of knowledge. Yellow and orange stand for the earth, from which a plant (the martial artist) takes root as the foundations of Tae Kwon Do are being built. Green symbolizes the plant's growth as Tae Kwon Do skills develop.

Blue stands for the sky toward which the plant reaches, maturing into a strong tree. Brown and red signify danger, cautioning the student to use control and warning others to stay away. Black is the opposite of white, symbolizing maturity and proficiency in Tae Kwon Do. It also stands for the wearer's ability to withstand darkness, fear and doubt.

The Black Belt

Black belt is the highest rank a student of Tae Kwon Do can achieve and requires several years of continuous study to earn. The black belt itself has varying degrees, called *dan*. In Tae Kwon Do, there are nine black belt dans. At the fifth dan (degree), a black belt is called "master." For black belts, to earn a dan requires a certain period of time as well as a certain amount of skill. For instance, to be eligible to test for the second dan black belt, one must have practiced for at least two years since earning the first dan black belt. The time necessary between dans increases at each level. This means that if you've been practicing for only three or four years, you might be a black belt but you can't be a third dan black belt. Thus, true dedication to the art must be shown before the higher black belt degrees are awarded. To earn the highest black belt levels, you must operate your own school, demonstrate that you are actively teaching the art to others, or show that you have somehow contributed significantly to the art.

Promotion Tests

Moving forward through the ranks, which each student is expected to do, is accomplished by successfully passing a promotion test, which usually requires the demonstration of fighting techniques, forms, sparring and board breaking. Several judges are usually present to evaluate the tests, which are offered every few months. Such tests are considered an important training tool, since they force the student to perform under conditions of pressure and stress. Schools set their own standards for passing tests, usually following criteria approved by the Tae Kwon Do style they follow, but the main goal is for each student to show good character and to strive to be the best martial artist he or she can be. In Tae Kwon Do, effort and attitude count for much more than mere ability.

Judging Your Own Progress

Rankings are sometimes very important to beginning martial artists, and especially if you are practicing alone, it can be discouraging to feel you are not making progress, or to be uncertain about whether you are or not. But in no other sport is attitude worth so much. Perseverance is rewarded, not just with physical benefits, but with mental rewards as well. Therefore, it is important to continue practicing no matter what.

To combat discouragement, keep a workout journal that tracks your accomplishments, including what techniques you've learned, how

A group of Tae Kwon Do students participate in a promotion test (left) as a panel of judges intently watches (right).

your conditioning has improved, and the like. Update the journal every few days and consult it regularly to judge your progress.

Tae Kwon Do Styles

There are several kinds of Tae Kwon Do, sometimes known as "styles." Often, these are designated by the name of their governing body, such as WTF-style, which is overseen by the World Tae Kwon Do Federation, or ITF-style, which is governed by the International Tae Kwon Do Federation. The two main differences among Tae Kwon Do styles are:

1. The forms that are taught (for example, ITF forms or Tae Geuk forms)
2. The way sparring is taught.

If you are taking lessons, it's a good idea to ask your instructor which style you are learning so that you don't invest in books or videos that teach you the wrong forms for your style. Tae Kwon Do practitioners routinely separate Tae Kwon Do styles into two groups, traditional and sport, also called Olympic style. If a Tae Kwon Do practitioner meets another person who studies Tae Kwon Do, the first question is often, "traditional or Olympic style?" This determines how the martial artist spars.

Olympic Style Tae Kwon Do

Olympic style Tae Kwon Do, of course, is the style seen at the Olympics. It emphasizes the sport side of Tae Kwon Do, in particular, sparring. Olympic style schools tend to place less emphasis on forms and board breaking. Thus, they practice freestyle sparring more than traditional schools do. The sparring method taught in Olympic style Tae Kwon Do emphasizes power more than speed. This is because a "trembling shock" must be applied to the opponent's body for a point to count. "Trembling shock," sometimes called "trembling blow," means the opponent must be visibly moved through space by the force of an unblocked technique for a point to be awarded. For this reason, sparring techniques tend to be limited to those few kicks that generate the most power, even if they aren't the quickest kicks. For example, an Olympic style fighter might rely mostly on backleg roundhouse kicks and reverse kicks, both to the midsection, because of the power of these kicks.

Traditional Style Tae Kwon Do

Traditional Tae Kwon Do schools place greater emphasis on the whole martial arts experience, with the practice of forms equally important to the practice of sparring. Formal etiquette is practiced and traditional uniforms are worn.

Traditional style sparring differs in that a point counts as long as a technique is unblocked and touches the other person. Therefore, traditional style sparring is usually lighter contact than Olympic style. Skill and technique are more important than power. For this reason, the quicker opponent often has the advantage, so power techniques are less important in sparring. A traditional style fighter will use front leg techniques, spinning wheel kicks and the like for speed. Power techniques, like the reverse kick and backleg roundhouse kick, are usually reserved to counter an opponent's attack, and are used far less frequently than in Olympic style sparring.

This Book's Approach

This book takes a traditional approach for several reasons. One important reason is that most students expect to be taught traditional style Tae Kwon Do. Unless they specifically want to learn Olympic style sparring, students usually think of traditional style Tae Kwon Do when they think of martial arts. Although they might never use a spinning wheel kick in an altercation, most students would like to learn how. Also, even if a student is learning or has learned Olympic style Tae Kwon Do, the information given here will still apply. That is, a straight punch is a straight punch, regardless of style. And even if a student prefers Olympic style sparring, the information in the sparring section will help improve his or her sparring skills. The drills that are suggested work well regardless of style. Finally, the form that is shown, *Chon-ji*, is a beginner form that all styles of Tae Kwon Do teach to white belts.

When using this book as a supplement to formal instruction, remember that your teacher is the final authority on what you should learn and how you should learn it.

Please remember that the practice of martial arts can be dangerous. Take the appropriate precautions when practicing. This book gives the information needed to practice basic and intermediate Tae Kwon Do, but all students of Tae Kwon Do are encouraged to seek professional instruction when available.

Whether you've practiced martial arts before, or are just starting out, whether you've been athletic in the past or haven't lifted anything heavier than a bag of groceries, with desire and practice, you can discover the meaning of martial arts by unlocking the secrets of Tae Kwon Do.

2

The History of Tae Kwon Do

Martial arts, as systems of combat, have been practiced for at least 4,000 years. Literature and art show martial artists and describe martial arts competitions. Asian folklore recounts how mythical creatures called Tengu practiced martial arts and taught their techniques to worthy humans. The founders of early martial arts styles would often claim the Tengu had taught them the art to add legitimacy to their systems.

Origins in India

Martial arts are thought to have developed in India, probably in connection with the religions and philosophies that were practiced there. From their origins in India, martial arts made their way throughout Asia over a period of centuries. According to legend, the Indian Buddhist monk Bodhidharma (460–534 A.D.) was responsible for the spread of martial arts. Bodhidharma, the founder of Zen Buddhism, left India to spread his religion. As he proselytized, he also taught martial arts to the monks he came in contact with, thus establishing the Shaolin Monastery, where he stayed, as the center of martial arts in China.

The Shaolin Temple

The Shaolin Temple is popularly called the birthplace of Asian martial arts. Originally located in the Hunan province high in the Sung-Shan mountain range, it was established in the late fifth century to honor the Buddhist monk Bodhiruchi. In the sixth century, Bodhidharma arrived. Although historians dispute whether he brought what we consider martial arts with him, the evidence suggests that he did bring with him a few principles of self-defense or at least some ideas about physical fitness.

The Shaolin Temple was the object of much interest from the government, especially since the temple gave refuge to rebels. Temples and monasteries often served as sanctuaries throughout much of Asian history, but Shaolin was a large, famous center and attracted many people for a variety of reasons (some devout, some not). Thus, the temple seemed a threat to the relatively unstable government of the region.

The temple was destroyed several times in raids and was eventually moved to Fukien province in the south. This so-called "Second Shaolin Temple" was also destroyed. Thereupon, the resident monks and nuns scattered again, this time for good. Popular belief suggests that as they moved through China and other parts of Asia, they taught Shaolin martial arts to others. Even now, martial arts systems claim to have descended from the Shaolin Temple to gain legitimacy.

Spread of Martial Arts Through China

Whether this legend is true or not, it is true that formal martial arts training schools were soon established throughout China. As the martial arts spread, they became not just methods of self-defense but also systems of fighting, even of attacking others. This is the side of martial arts that warriors such as the Japanese Samurai embraced. The Samurai followed a strict code of conduct and promised undying loyalty to their overlords, but they could also be aggressive and murderous.

Commoners used martial arts to protect themselves and their property from thieves and other threats. The weapons they used were developed from everyday tools. For example, the tonfa fighting stick developed from the handle of a grinding tool. The famous Karate nunchuks were originally flails used to separate rice. Staffs were walking sticks converted to deadly weapons. Such weapons were necessary because commoners and other subject people were frequently forbidden to use or own typical weapons, such as swords.

Higher-born individuals learned martial arts that included the use of swords and other high-class weapons. Men, women and children of all classes learned martial arts; even now, martial arts training is the most popular sport in Asia.

Origins of Tae Kwon Do

Tae Kwon Do itself developed in Korea from Chinese origins. Originally, empty-hand (weaponless) fighting systems came to Korea from T'ang Dynasty China. This is known because mid-seventh century artwork, such as sculptures, show martial arts techniques being used in Korea. These martial arts techniques are similar to what was being used in T'ang Dynasty China. It is also known that China and Korea had considerable contact during this period.

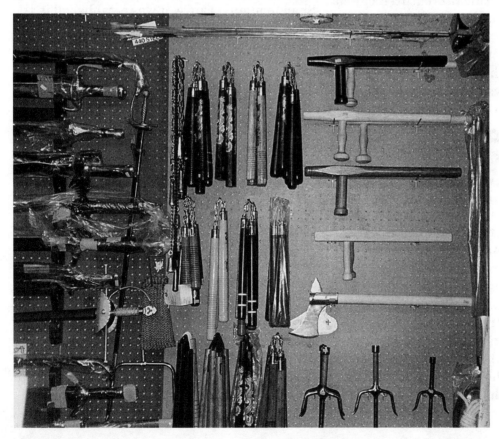

Martial arts weapons include nunchuks, tonfa and sai.

Subak and Tae Kyun, early Korean martial arts, were learned by warriors who participated in martial tournaments. At this time, there were three kingdoms in Korea — Silla, Koguryo and Baekje. The Silla Kingdom eventually became quite powerful. As it did so, a group of noble youths who prepared for military leadership sprang up. Called the *Hwarang,* or "flowering youth," they became important figures in Silla Dynasty Korea, like the Samurai of feudal Japan. *Hwarang-do,* "the way of flowering youth," was the curriculum taught to these young men. Martial strategy, Buddhism, etiquette, arts and sciences were all taught, as were the three main qualities of Hwarang-do: loyalty, courage and justice.

Won Kang Bopsa, a Buddhist monk, is credited with creating the martial art Tae Kyun, which he taught to the Hwarang. Although it was primarily a method of training and conditioning at first, it became a method of fighting influenced by both Chinese and Japanese martial arts.

Martial Arts in the Koryo Dynasty

In Korea, training in the martial arts was mandatory for higher-ranking individuals until the 10th century, when the Koryo Dynasty was founded. It was from this dynasty that the name Korea ("Koryo") was given to the country. During the Koryo Dynasty, Confucianism supplanted Buddhism as the dominant philosophical/spiritual belief. Confucianism downplayed martial arts and martial achievements and instead celebrated cultural and intellectual achievements. Thus, the study of martial arts in Korea began to decline.

Effects of the Mongol Invasion

Subsequent to the Korean loss of interest in martial ways, the warlike Mongols found it easy to invade in the 13th century. Though Mongol domination ended in the next century, Korea continued to suffer internal turmoil and decline. The Yi Dynasty was established, but, like the Koryo Dynasty, it

too emphasized culture and learning at the expense of martial arts. During this period, Korean warriors — who found themselves persecuted and unwelcome — took refuge in Buddhist temples. There, they taught their martial arts privately to a select few. Korea struggled along with some assistance from China, but it never regained its former power and influence.

The Hermit Kingdom

When Japan invaded in 1592, Korea was poorly prepared, but China helped it to oust the Japanese. Over the next decades, Korea closed itself off to the outside world. Because of this, it was known for many years as "The Hermit Kingdom." Only the Chinese were permitted easy access to Korea, and the country tried to shut itself away from other outside influences.

In the early 20th century, Japan fought China for control of Korea. The Japanese conquest of Korea in 1903 was a part of the Russo-Japanese War. Korea was occupied by Japan until the end of World War II. During their occupation, the Japanese banned Koreans from practicing the martial arts, but many still did so secretly. Unlike other cultures that developed ways to use weapons even when they were banned (such as the Okinawans who developed nunchuks from farming tools), for the most part, Korean martial artists did not incorporate weapons into their fighting systems. Instead, they developed spectacular empty-hand-and-foot techniques to combat the enemy, whether armed or unarmed. These techniques were passed along in secret.

Korean Independence

After Korea gained independence from Japan, Korean martial artists became interested in systematizing the various Korean martial arts techniques. General Hong-Hi Choi is generally credited as the founder of modern Tae Kwon Do, for he spearheaded the efforts to develop a modern version of Korean martial arts. General Choi had been imprisoned by the Japanese for inciting Koreans to rebel. After independence, he became a martial arts instructor in the Korean armed forces. As a well-respected military figure, he brought legitimacy and common sense to the efforts to consolidate Korean martial arts under one system.

Tae Kwon Do master Jhoon Rhee introduced Tae Kwon Do to the United States in the late 1950s. It was considered a form of Karate for a long time, mostly because Americans recognized what Karate was but had not heard of Tae Kwon Do. In the 1980s, American Tae Kwon Do practitioners began making special efforts to increase the recognition of the martial art, and now it is nearly as popular as Karate.

Outside Influences on Tae Kwon Do

Tae Kwon Do has always emphasized training both the mind and body. Its unique characteristics can be traced to its roots. The flashy high kicks and jumping kicks, for which Tae Kwon Do is best known, were developed to strike at mounted warriors during the Korean feudal period. The circular movements, joint locks, breathing exercises and some throwing techniques are Chinese in character while the striking techniques and vital point attacks are influenced by the Japanese martial arts.

By wedding these various influences to their traditional martial arts techniques, Korean martial artists developed a challenging, fascinating system of combat that encompasses more than personal self-defense.

3

Benefits of Tae Kwon Do

Training in Tae Kwon Do has many benefits, both physical and mental. That's why it appeals to people of all ages, sizes and physical conditions. No matter where you are now, you can become better — healthier, more fit and less stressed. Older people have successfully trained in the martial arts. Many sixty-, seventy- and even eighty-year-olds practice Tae Kwon Do. Young people also gain from practicing Tae Kwon Do. Students as young as four or five years old have been taught the rudiments of self-defense as well as basic ethics. For adults, no matter their physical condition, Tae Kwon Do can improve all areas of life.

Physical disabilities do not preclude participation. Individuals in wheelchairs have practiced Tae Kwon Do, as have those who suffer from conditions such as cystic fibrosis, multiple sclerosis and different kinds of arthritis. Many such individuals have benefitted greatly from their participation in the martial arts, both physically and mentally.

Students of all ages, shapes and sizes practice Tae Kwon Do.

Power, Strength, Flexibility and Endurance

The consistent practice of Tae Kwon Do can help you develop power, strength, flexibility and endurance. Once you learn how to do the techniques, with practice, you can make these workouts aerobic, which will effectively increase your lung capacity and improve your overall cardiovascular health.

15

Martial arts practice helps develop strength and flexibility for the purpose of self-defense and general fitness. Flexibility is needed for many of the techniques in Tae Kwon Do, including the high kicks and jumping kicks. But even if you don't start out with great flexibility, you can achieve it. This flexibility is useful in everyday life, making ordinary tasks easier and preventing strains and sprains that often happen when your body is stiff, sore and out of shape.

Strength is gained through continual practice of techniques, forms and sparring. This is one way that the emphasis on repetition of techniques improves your fitness level. Many martial artists also lift weights to add to their strength, but this is not necessary. Most new practitioners see a significant increase in strength and muscle tone within the first few months of training.

Self-Confidence

Learning self-defense techniques can make you feel confident and more courageous — willing to take chances and opportunities in your martial arts practice. This self-confidence can help you become more assertive and stronger in all parts of life. In addition, because practicing Tae Kwon Do improves fitness and can lead to weight loss, it helps people feel more self-confident about their physical appearance. In fact, it often teaches people to appreciate strength and fitness, not some impossible ideal that rail-thin fashion models promote. Martial artists learn that frailty is not beautiful, and this leads to a better self-image.

Self-Discipline

Accomplishing martial arts skills also leads to feelings of control and mastery. As you continue training, you learn self-discipline. In order to keep the skills and techniques fresh in mind, it's important to do them repeatedly. Repetition also helps train your body to be able to do the techniques almost effortlessly. To continue practice, discipline is required. To work on your skills even when you're tired further develops discipline.

Then, too, you will need to learn self-discipline and self-control in other areas of life so that you can succeed at Tae Kwon Do. For example, if you want to be strong and flexible to perform the techniques, you may need to lose weight. Or, to have the energy to practice after a long day of work, you may need to eat better or get more sleep. All of this helps you to become a more self-disciplined person.

Focus and Concentration

Tae Kwon Do also teaches focus and concentration. Learning to do the techniques correctly and executing them perfectly requires your full attention. For this reason, a martial arts workout is an excellent antidote to a stressful day. But focus and concentration don't come immediately. They are learned with practice. Focus and concentration are required when you try to practice despite interruptions, and when you put off doing other activities you may enjoy so that you can practice Tae Kwon Do.

Chi

One of the greatest benefits you will get from practicing Tae Kwon Do is inner energy. This energy is called *chi* (sometimes spelled *ki* or *qi*). Some martial artists believe *chi* is equivalent to a life force that can be controlled and directed at opponents; in this way, it is a mystical force that you can learn to use. Others think of *chi* simply as the ability to focus your energy on a specific goal. The yell or shout that you hear martial artists use helps focus the artist's energy and attention while he or she performs a difficult technique. This yell, called a *kihop*, comes from the abdomen or solar plexus and is developed as part of controlled breathing exercises that most martial arts teach. These breathing exercises also help relieve stress and calm you down. How to develop *chi* is discussed in Chapter 5.

4

The Tenets of Tae Kwon Do

The ultimate goal of Tae Kwon Do training is the development of qualities that make you a better person. All Tae Kwon Do students are expected to learn and follow the Five Tenets of Tae Kwon Do. These are qualities or principles by which Tae Kwon Do practitioners are expected to live. As a system of ethical behavior, they are considered important to the development of character. Although they are easy to memorize, the Tenets are not so easy to understand. Part of the process of living the way of Tae Kwon Do is to appreciate how to use the Tenets not just in the training hall but in everyday life.

Although each of the Tenets identifies a separate characteristic, they are interrelated. Practicing one requires practicing them all. It is not possible to pick and choose which Tenets to adhere to.

The Tenets

The Five Tenets of Tae Kwon Do are courtesy, integrity, perseverance, self-control and indomitable spirit. Although it is expected that the martial artist will practice these tenets in all areas of life — home, work, school, etc. — they are practiced in specific ways in the dojang

or training hall. This practice benefits martial artists outside of the hall as they learn to understand how to apply these principles in everyday life.

The Five Tenets

17

Courtesy

Courtesy helps create an environment where ego does not reign supreme. In a classroom setting, courtesy is shown by bowing to the instructor and other classmates and by calling instructors and higher ranking students "sir" or "ma'am." Courtesy is also shown by addressing more experienced martial artists by their title and last name, such as "Mr. Smith" or "Sa Beum Nim Smith." Courtesy requires that you share your knowledge with others. It also means treating the art itself with respect, by not using it unnecessarily or boasting about your martial arts achievements.

Courtesy outside the training hall is a little more than simply practicing good manners. It is also a way of looking at the world. For example, if someone is rude to you, your first reaction might be to act rudely in return. But if you are practicing courtesy, you will try not to be rude. However, you may still be angered by the other person's rudeness. True courtesy demands that you learn to rethink such situations so that you don't waste valuable energy becoming angry in the first place. True courtesy means you not only ignore other people's discourtesy, but are unaffected by it.

Integrity

Integrity is the way in which you conduct your dealings with others. It is, essentially, a commitment to honest and ethical behavior. In the training hall, this means working out as hard as you can each time you train. It means putting your greatest effort into each technique and movement, even if no one is watching what you are doing. Instead of offering excuses for why you can't work as hard as you should, it means being committed to practicing as perfectly as possible every time.

Outside the training hall, there are countless opportunities to show integrity. At work, you should put forth your best effort each day even if you're mad at the boss and don't really feel like working. It means you should be accountable to your loved ones at all times, never lying or misrepresenting anything to them. It also means being honest with yourself, so that you don't cheat yourself of opportunities to grow and learn.

Perseverance

Perseverance is the unwillingness to give up, even if a task seems too difficult to do. It requires that you continue to try even if you have been unsuccessful in the past. If, for example, a technique is difficult to do, one doesn't just abandon it and move on to the next one. It means working until you can do the technique as it was intended. Sometimes this can take weeks and even months of persistence, but you cannot let frustration and discouragement prevent you from accomplishing your martial arts goals.

The same exercise of perseverance can help you succeed outside the dojang or training hall by helping you pursue your own personal or career goals or dreams through continual effort and hard work.

Self-Control

Self-control has to do with the control of your physical body and control of your emotions. It requires you to restrain both physical and mental reactions, using reason and judgment, not fear or anger, to make decisions. It is a matter of discipline. Control over the body helps one learn control over emotions, which leads to a healthier, less stressful life and environment.

Self-control requires that you control your emotions and carefully consider how you respond to others. In the training hall, self-control is also a matter of using willpower to stay fit even if it means turning down a night on the town or your favorite fast-food lunch.

Self-control means controlling emotions of fear so that you may overcome them and succeed in your training. It is controlling feelings of frustration and disappointment so that you remain courteous at all times. When working with others, control means you will keep from overpowering your partners even if you can easily do so. For example, if you are sparring a person less skilled than you, you don't need to take advantage of every opening or spar so hard that your partner becomes humiliated and frustrated. While it is natural to wish to win or do your best, it is not necessary to embarrass others while doing so.

Indomitable Spirit

Finally, indomitable spirit is having the right attitude whether you win or lose. Having a positive or cheerful outlook helps get you through the tough times. It's the attitude that inspires you to compete against yourself and others, but also to remain upbeat, focused and undiscouraged even if you fail. Indomitable spirit is the realization that participating in the martial arts is not about winning or losing, but about the process of preparing and learning. If you have indomitable spirit, you cannot be beaten even if you lose a match or do poorly in a competition. That fact that you participated in a match or took the opportunity to compete in a tournament says more about you and your spirit than winning or losing does.

Indomitable spirit helps you to remain optimistic outside the training hall as well. Instead of approaching life in a cynical, pessimistic way, one is able to keep a positive mental balance that makes handling the challenges of daily life a little easier.

The Secret of Tae Kwon Do

The real secret to Tae Kwon Do is trying to make a deliberate, conscious effort to follow the Five Tenets. Following this ethical system makes a Tae Kwon Do practitioner a better martial artist and a better person. By practicing the Five Tenets, you learn to create balance and harmony in your life by creating balance and harmony between your body and your mind. When this harmony is disrupted, it is easy to become unhappy and confused. Through cultivation of courtesy, integrity, perseverance, self-control and indomitable spirit, it is possible to lead a satisfying, integrated life.

5

Developing Chi
and Winning Spirit

One of the greatest benefits of Tae Kwon Do is the development of *chi*, or inner energy. Being able to focus on and use this inner energy improves your martial arts skills.

Martial artists attempt to summon chi by shouting. This is called the *kihop*. Correct use of chi can make you more powerful, focused and determined. Focusing all of one's energy on a single target, goal or task requires practice and concentration. As you practice Tae Kwon Do techniques, you should try to do each technique perfectly each time you attempt it. By concentrating on exactly what your body is doing, you will discipline your mind to focus. Adding the yell or kihop as you do the technique helps you generate the energy you need to do it well. How to develop a good kihop is discussed later in the chapter.

Winning Spirit

Chi is essential to winning spirit, which is important to success in the martial arts. Winning spirit is another way of saying "indomitable spirit," which is one of the Tenets of Tae Kwon Do. In addition to developing chi, other qualities are important to developing winning spirit and to becoming the best martial artist possible.

Fudoshin

One of these necessary qualities is *fudoshin*, a Japanese term which means the ability to remain calm and detached when confronted with a threat or difficulty. If you can remain calm and in control, you'll be less concerned about personal harm and risk. By reducing fear and confusion, you'll be able to make good decisions, reacting with a clear and open mind. You won't panic and make poor decisions. Fudoshin is a manifestation of self-control.

Heijo-Shin

One must have *fudoshin* to develop *heijo-shin*, which is intense focus. An intensely focused mind is essential to preparing for and coping with any great challenge. Some martial artists say they can see when another person has focus or heijo-shin. Developing this ability helps one to remain alert and ready, which reduces fear, surprise and indecision.

Kokoro

Fudoshin and heijo-shin—self-control and focus—are necessary for tests of all kinds, and are developed through meditation and through physical exercise. But these mental attitudes are nothing without heart or spirit. You can have great martial art talent but without *kokoro*, which is heart or spirit, you will ultimately fail. A martial artist without heart is not a true martial artist. A person with kokoro will many times defeat a person who has greater skills but no heart. Kokoro, in the end, comes from doing your best and giving your best effort at all times. Kokoro is the manifestation of perseverance and indomitable spirit, of having heart whatever the situation.

Yin-Yang

Understanding the concept of yin-yang (called *um-yang* in Korean) helps a martial artist achieve balance. Yin-yang is a concept that describes how the universe works. It states that all creation consists of conflicting but nonetheless harmonious elements that depend on each other for their meaning. For example, hot and cold have no meaning except in their relationship to one another.

Yin symbolizes the destructive elements in the universe, plus those things characterized as passive and feminine. *Yang* symbolizes the creative elements in the universe, plus those things characterized as active and masculine. These opposites are necessary and combine to make a whole. Therefore, the martial artist must combine the hard and the soft, the passive and the active, to become the best martial artist possible. Understanding yin-yang also requires that you practice moderation in all things.

Effects of Chi and Winning Spirit

Fear, doubt and confusion all work to defeat the martial artist. All of these problems and emotions are the result of the martial artist's own attitude. Through dedicated practice of the martial arts, you can learn to eliminate these destructive beliefs and encourage creative, constructive beliefs and attitudes.

Meditation

The martial arts also emphasize techniques of meditation, which are methods for focusing your thoughts, visualizing self-improvement, or reflecting on spiritual or religious issues. Many Asian religions and philosophies encourage the use of meditation for achieving enlightenment.

Zazen meditation is a form of meditation in which the goal is simply to control and stop all thoughts, trying to attain an empty, harmonious mind. Many martial arts, including Tae Kwon Do, teach this type of meditation. Sometimes it is taken a step further and visualization is practiced, in which you empty your mind and then consider the aspects of your martial arts performance that could be improved. This is somewhat different from *satori*, or meditation that leads to enlightenment, which is attempted in Zen Buddhism.

Breathing Techniques

To facilitate meditation and even just to improve focus, Tae Kwon Do practitioners use various types of breathing. The breathing technique most frequently used by beginners is to

Pausing during the workout to focus breathe is called "chareyhet breathing."

inhale deeply through the nose, then exhale slowly through the mouth. Your breath should go deep into your stomach. Your chest *and* your abdomen should move in and out. Doing this breathing after a workout or at intervals throughout a workout helps your body by making sure enough oxygen is delivered. You can increase your stamina and endurance by incorporating such breathing techniques into your workouts. In addition, concentrating on your breathing can help you focus at other times, such as when you are under a deadline at work or are otherwise faced with a stressful situation.

Focused breathing technique can also be used to control your breathing by deliberately slowing your breath rate, which helps you to recover more quickly from physical exertion. It also helps you control stress by calming you down. As you breathe, take a few seconds longer to inhale and exhale between breaths, gradually extending the length of time between breaths until you are relaxed and can breathe slowly without effort.

Tae Kwon Do students must learn to be aware of their breathing at all times. When practicing techniques, you breathe out while striking with the technique. This helps add focus and power to each technique. Then, inhale when returning to the starting position. As Tae Kwon Do students become more comfortable with their breathing, they notice improved endurance. This breathing is most easily accomplished if you concentrate on exhaling as you strike. Inhaling will then naturally follow. Don't breathe too rapidly or you'll hyperventilate.

One secret to breathing for relaxation is to extend your arms out to the side while inhaling, to increase lung capacity. Slowly push your hands together while exhaling. Imagine the breath coming into and leaving your lungs as you do this.

Developing a Strong Kihop

Breathing exercises will also help you learn to yell. *Kihop* is the term Tae Kwon Do practitioners use for the yell that focuses their energy. The kihop is used when executing techniques, and during sparring and board breaking. Although you needn't kihop with every technique, it's important to learn how. The kihop helps focus your thoughts and energy on the task at

Push Hands Together Breathing Technique: Inhale deeply and extend arms to the side, then push hands together while slowly exhaling.

hand. You might, for example, practice your kihop by using it for the first five techniques of your workout, or after every set of techniques during step sparring. It doesn't matter how you practice it so long as you practice it.

Take some time to experiment with different yells. Keep them short but powerful. A good kihop is a solid shout (not a scream) that carries conviction. It should originate in the abdomen — the solar plexus. To locate the solar plexus, try exhaling slowly. With three fingers, push your abdomen in, two or three inches above your navel. You should feel the difference in your breathing. Concentrate on starting the shout from that part of the body.

Through practice, meditation and breathing, you will be able to develop chi, intense focus and winning spirit.

The solar plexus is located below the ribs and slightly above the navel.

Part II

6

Warm-Ups and Stretches

What to Wear

Ordinarily, students practice or work out in uniforms purchased for this purpose. The Tae Kwon Do uniform is called a *dobok*. Tae Kwon Do practitioners usually work out in their bare feet, because this conditions their feet to withstand the physical stress of kicking and performing footwork. Also, it is difficult to learn how to pivot and turn while wearing shoes. Once the principle of pivoting is understood, Tae Kwon Do practitioners sometimes vary their routine by working out in shoes to get a feel for it. Shoes should always be worn when practicing outdoors or on uneven surfaces. If you do wear shoes, you should invest in specially designed martial arts shoes which are lightweight and have a pivot point at the ball of the foot.

Although it isn't necessary to wear a uniform when working out on your own, it can be a good idea to do so. First, by wearing a neat, clean uniform each time you practice, you show respect for yourself and for Tae Kwon Do. Dirty, wrinkled uniforms suggest you don't

A wide variety of workout clothing is available to martial artists.

care about how you look and more importantly, you don't care about the art. The uniform is a symbol of the art. Second, the uniform reminds you as you work out that you are a martial artist. This thought helps you to persevere. Sometimes you need to be reminded not to give up or settle for less than a perfect effort. Wearing the uniform reminds you that the art is bigger than you are, and that you are following in a tradition of strong individuals who would be disappointed should you give up. Finally, the act of changing into the uniform helps you to become mentally ready for your workout. By shedding your street clothes and assuming the Tae Kwon Do uniform, you shed the concerns and stresses of the outside world and get your mind ready for your workout. This helps you to focus and concentrate on the task at hand, which is practicing Tae Kwon Do to the best of your ability.

What to Avoid

When practicing the martial arts, it's important to remember safety at all times. For this reason, you should never wear jewelry of any kind while practicing. This includes necklaces, earrings, engagement and wedding rings and the like. It is very easy to snag your jewelry as you're kicking and punching. Also, if you work with a partner, he or she could get hurt by coming into contact with jewelry. For safety reasons, you should wear contact lenses instead of glasses. Not only can glass lenses shatter, but the frames and hinges can be dangerous. Also, if a heavy bag or a partner accidentally knocks your glasses against your head, you could get seriously injured. If contact lenses are not practical or possible, wear glasses especially designed for use in sports. Or, if your eyesight isn't that bad, avoid wearing glasses altogether.

In addition, don't wear makeup while practicing martial arts. It runs, gets on your clothes, and, if you sweat much, will get into your eyes. Keep your nails trimmed close — not just your fingernails but your toenails as well. It's easy to cut yourself or a partner, or to catch and pull a nail. Plus, you can't make a proper fist if your fingernails are too long.

Purchasing Uniforms and Shoes

Uniforms and shoes can be purchased through local martial arts supply stores, or you can order them through the mail from martial arts supply houses. These national supply houses will send catalogs at your request:

American Martial Arts Supply
2968 West Ina Road, Building #136
Tucson, AZ 85741
Telephone: (800) 556-6238

Century Martial Arts Supply, Inc.
1705 National Boulevard
Midwest City, OK 73110
Telephone: (405) 732-2226 or (800) 626-2787

Macho Products, Inc.
10045 102nd Terrace
Sebastien, FL 32958
Telephone: (800) 327-6812

Pil Sung Martial Art Supply
6300 Ridglea Place, Suite 1008
Fort Worth, TX 76116
Telephone: (817) 738-5408

If you are practicing on your own and choose not to wear a dobok, wear loose-fitting, comfortable clothing. Nothing should tug or bind as you perform your techniques. However, you will want to keep shirts tucked in so they don't catch on anything as you work out.

Where to Practice

When practicing on your own, you will want to choose the right kind of area. First, you'll need at least an eight-by-eight-foot section of unobstructed space to practice your techniques, sparring and forms. Since Tae Kwon Do is practiced without shoes, you should practice on a carpeted area, or on a smooth wood floor. It is easier to perform the techniques on carpet because your feet slide with less effort, but practicing on different surfaces is actually a practical method of learning how to do the different techniques on different terrain. Therefore, practicing outdoors is also a good (and fun) change from working out in the basement. If you plan to practice outdoors, try to find an area that is fairly smooth and level and remove any objects, such as stones and sticks, that you could trip over or step on. It's a good idea to wear shoes when practicing outdoors. Bare concrete floors are very hard on your body and should be avoided if at all possible. At the minimum, invest in a square of padded carpet to put down on top of bare concrete.

What You'll Need

All you really need to practice Tae Kwon Do is yourself, some comfortable clothes and this book. But there are certain aids and pieces of equipment that you may consider investing in to help you get the most from your training. The uniform and martial arts shoes, as mentioned above, are always wise purchases. For practicing techniques and sparring, a heavy bag is a great investment. Many martial artists eventually purchase hanging heavy bags (you can attach them to a ceiling joist in the garage or basement) because of the workout you can get using one. The hanging heavy bag is the best choice of heavy bags because it is less likely to cause injury and has a better range of motion than other types of bags. But a hanging heavy bag is not a good idea if you're renting, plan to move soon or don't have a lot of room. There are freestanding heavy bags on the market that you don't have to hook into the ceiling. They can be easily moved out of the way when you're finished. If you have $100 and are wondering what your best martial arts investment is, a heavy bag is it.

Freestanding heavy bags can be a wise investment for apartment dwellers.

A big wall mirror or freestanding mirror that reflects your whole body is a great aid for making certain you are doing techniques correctly. By the same token, a video camera (borrow one if you don't own one) can help you see what you're doing and where you can make improvements.

Target bags and focus mitts can be purchased inexpensively through martial arts supply houses (see previous list). Cushions and pillows can sometimes be used as a substitute.

If you're sparring with partners, invest in sparring equipment (also called safety gear or

A target bag helps you put power in your kicks.

A focus mitt helps you make accurate strikes.

Sparring equipment helps prevent injuries.

safety equipment). This protects both you and your partner from unintentional bumps, scratches and bruises.

Finally, if you plan to practice takedown and throwing techniques with a partner, invest in a mat (called a *tatami*) to cover the floor. This will help prevent injuries.

Length of Workout

It's a good idea to practice some of your techniques every day just so that you don't forget them. Also, stretching exercises can be done at any time. The more you stretch, the better your flexibility will become. But for full-fledged workouts, think three or four times a week with a day off in between workouts. More often is fine, but don't overdo it and cause an injury. Sometimes martial artists burn out if they work too enthusiastically at first.

A thorough workout consists of warming up, stretching, techniques practice, forms practice, self-defense practice, sparring and cooling down. Allow at least ten minutes for warming up and stretching and at least five minutes cooling down for each session. Spend about fifteen minutes practicing techniques, especially at the beginning when you are learning many new ones. Next, allow five minutes for practicing Chon-ji form, ten minutes for self-defense practice and ten minutes for sparring. Following this sched-

ule allows you to complete a total Tae Kwon Do workout in about an hour. By spending a specifically allotted amount of time on each of the four stages, you will be more likely to develop into a balanced martial artist. Plus, you'll be learning the stages at more equal rates as well. By limiting the practice of each stage to between five and fifteen minutes, you will also eliminate any chance of boredom during practice. There will always be plenty of variety by adding in new fighting techniques, drills and the like.

As you continue your Tae Kwon Do practice, you may wish to vary the time you spend on each stage somewhat, and you may want to spend longer at your practice. Just remember to keep practicing all four stages, and don't overdo training until you know how much your body is fit for.

Warming Up

Once you're in your uniform or workout clothes, you'll need to warm up before you actually begin working on your techniques. Novice martial artists commonly complain of muscle pulls, strains and tears, almost all of which can be prevented with adequate warm-up and stretching exercises.

Start with a basic warm-up technique, such as a brisk walk or jog. Even jumping rope for a couple of minutes will help your body prepare for a more vigorous workout. When you notice an increased heart rate and breathing and a light film of sweat, you're ready to stretch.

Stretching

Stretching is an important part of Tae Kwon Do, since Tae Kwon Do requires flexibility for its high kicks. Stretching helps you gain the agility you need to succeed. Even if you are already flexible, you'll want to stretch anyway to maintain your flexibility and to prevent damage to your muscles. Tight, rigid muscles are prone to tears and strains. Loose, elastic muscle will stretch instead of tear.

What order you do your stretches in doesn't really matter, but starting from the head down is a good idea — then you don't miss a muscle group and wake up the next morning with a sore hamstring.

For all stretches, hold each for ten to thirty seconds. Don't try to get a better stretch by bouncing. You should feel the stretch, but no pain. If you feel pain, stop what you're doing immediately.

Give yourself at least five minutes for stretching before you start your workout. Ten minutes is even better.

Special Concerns

If you have arthritis in a joint or are recovering from an injury, make certain to spend extra time warming up that muscle area. Conditions such as carpal tunnel syndrome also require special attention during warming up. If you have such a condition, you should consider wearing a support for protection. ACE-type wraps aren't very useful for working out in — they can be wrapped too tightly, they get wet and they don't stay in place when you're moving around. Invest instead in a neoprene support or a cloth-and-rubber brace. These are available at many pharmacies, sporting goods stores and at medical supply houses. Some types of supports, such as lumbar support belts and carpal tunnel braces, are easy to find at office supply companies, since many businesses need these for their employees.

Cooling Down

When you've finished your workout, don't just stop and sit down. Make sure you have a cooling down period. This will help prevent muscle soreness and stiffness. You can do the stretches you did at the beginning of your workout, or you can do some light walking or jogging. Some martial artists practice their techniques slowly and gently during the cool down period, working on making their form perfect instead of worrying about power and speed.

You may find or develop your own set of stretches that you like to use, but following the stretches described below will warm up all the major muscle groups. Remember to spend a few minutes walking or jogging before you begin stretching.

Stretching is a good way to cool down after a workout.

Neck Rotation

To loosen up neck muscles, rotate your head back and forth. Or, to avoid pinching any nerves (if your neck and shoulders are especially tight), stretch your neck in each of the four directions. Tuck your chin toward your chest until you feel the stretch. Hold this position for 10 or 15 seconds. Then, hold your head to the left, tilting it as close to the shoulder as you can. Hold this position for 10 or 15 seconds. Next, hold your head to the right, keeping the position for 10 or 15 seconds. Lastly, look up toward the ceiling, feeling the back of your head touch your back. Hold for 10 or 15 seconds. Once you have stretched in the four directions, relax and repeat two or three times.

Shoulder Stretch

Swing your arms out from the side. Then reach toward the ceiling, stretching your arms up as much as possible. Hold the stretch for 10 to 15 seconds.

Arm Rotation

Swing your arms up in front of you, making a circle from front to back. Repeat 10 times.

Wrist Stretch

To loosen your wrist and hand, extend your arm slightly in front of your body. Keeping your palm open, pull your fingers back. Hold for 10 to 15 seconds. Repeat five times for each hand.

Back Stretch

In a seated position, stretch your legs out in front of you. Reach forward with your hands, trying to touch the tips of your toes. Keep your legs straight — don't bend your knees. Don't overdo it and don't bounce. Hold the position for 15 seconds, then relax and repeat two more times.

Hip/Groin Stretch

In a seated position, extend your legs straight out in front of you. Then slide your feet toward you, bending your knees, until the soles of your feet are touching and your knees are out to the side. Continue moving your legs toward you until you feel a good stretch. Hold the position for 10 seconds. Then, for a further stretch, lean forward, trying to touch your forehead to your feet. Hold this position for 10 seconds. Repeat.

Hamstring Stretch

Sit on the floor, legs stretched out in front. Pull one knee toward your chest until you feel the stretch. Hold for 10 to 15 seconds. Repeat five times for each leg.

Hip Stretch

Bend your knee and rotate your leg in a circle, moving your leg out from the front to the side slowly. Then rotate your bent leg from the side back to the front. Repeat this rotation several times for both legs, moving slowly and gently at first and then moving with greater speed as you warm up the hip area. If you need support, stand near a wall and place your palm on the wall.

Quadriceps Stretch

Stand near a wall, putting your hands on the wall for support. Extend your leg straight out behind you, lifting it as high as you can. Don't bend your knee. Hold in this position for 15 seconds. Repeat five times on each leg.

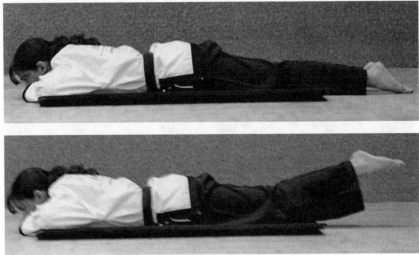

Thigh Stretch

Lying on your stomach, place your arms under your head. Use a mat for comfort. Lift both legs about 12 inches off the floor. Hold for 15 seconds. Relax and repeat.

Calf Raises

Standing straight, lift your heels off the ground until you are standing on your toes. (Place your palms against a wall if you find it hard to keep your balance). Hold this stretch for 10 seconds. Then lower your heels to the ground and rock back until your toes are off the ground. Hold this stretch for 10 seconds. Then repeat five times.

Ankle Rotation

In a seated position, cross your legs. Lifting the top leg slightly, rotate your foot in all directions. Use your hand to help stretch your ankle. Do several rotations with each ankle, starting very slowly and gently and going faster as you repeat the stretch.

Remember that proper stretching is essential. You may discover other stretches that you prefer to use, and by all means incorporate them into your stretching routine. But don't forget to warm up and stretch before each Tae Kwon Do workout.

7

Basic and Intermediate Stances *(Ja Sae)*

Stances are the body positions from which martial arts techniques are performed. They provide balance for defense or attacks. Stances are primarily about the placement of your feet and, secondarily, the placement of your arms. Although most techniques can be performed in any stance, the differences among the stances are important to learn.

Ready Stance (Chunbee)

The first stance is the ready stance. This is the position you take before beginning your workout and before beginning a form. The Korean term for *ready* is *chunbee*, so this is sometimes called the *chunbee* stance.

Ready Stance

Stand with your feet comfortably apart, and your back straight. Make your hands into fists and bend your arms about 45 degrees. Hold your arms slightly away from your body and look directly ahead.

Attention Stance (Chareyhet)

The attention stance is used to show courtesy and respect to others. In a formal class, students come to the attention stance when speaking to an instructor or any higher ranking belt. The Korean word for attention is *chareyhet*, so this is sometimes called the *chareyhet* stance. The attention stance is performed by placing the feet together so that the inner edges are touching. Arms should be held stiffly at the side, slightly away from the body. Hands can be made into fists or held open. Your eyes should be forward, looking directly ahead. Nothing should distract you from the attention position.

Horse Stance (Kim Ja Sae)

The horse stance, sometimes called the horseback stance or the riding horse stance, is common to almost all martial arts styles. Many of the basic hand techniques are practiced from

In the attention stance, the feet are together so that the inner edges touch and arms are held stiffly, slightly away from the body.

Front Stance (*Chongul Ja Sae*)

The front stance, also called the forward stance, is used frequently in Tae Kwon Do. It is performed by facing the front and placing one leg forward, bending the knee at a 90-degree angle, and placing the other leg to the back. The back leg is kept straight; both heels should be touching the floor. The lower you make the front leg, the better the stance. Elbows are bent at the side and hands are made into fists.

An exaggerated front stance with a long distance between the front and back legs is called *notchwoh sae*. This stance is used for thrusting strikes, such as the *kwansu*, or spear hand strike. It is also a good technique for building strong leg muscles.

A short front stance, called *pahn chun ja sae*, is performed by moving the front and rear leg closer together and reducing the angle of the bend of the front knee. This stance is used to perform overhead or high strikes, such as the backfist strike and the hammer fist strike. It can also be used as a type of fighting stance during freestyle sparring.

Back Stance (*Hugul Ja Sae*)

The back stance is a side-facing stance. With your head forward but your body facing to the side, place your front foot slightly forward, bending the knee and keeping the heel off the floor. The back foot should be placed at a 90 degree angle to the front foot. The back leg should be bent. Most of your

this stance. It is performed by facing forward and placing the feet parallel to each other, about a shoulder's width and a half apart. Bend the knees so that the thigh and calf meet at a 90-degree angle. Elbows are bent at the side and hands are made into fists. The lower you can keep your body, the better the stance. A stance that is held low is called a "strong stance."

Horse Stance (left): Many basic hand techniques are performed in the horse stance.

To properly execute the front stance, place one foot forward, bending the knee 90 degrees. Place the other leg to the back, keeping it straight. Both legs should be about a shoulder's width apart. Both heels should touch the floor.

weight should be on your back leg (80 percent). This way the front leg can quickly block or strike.

Back Stance: Look forward, but turn the chest and hips to the side. The front foot should be forward from the body, knee bent 45 degrees. The back foot should be at a 90-degree angle to the front foot, heels perpendicular to each other. Back knee should be bent close to 90 degrees. The heel of the front foot should be lifted off the ground, with the back leg bearing most of the weight.

Fighting Stance (Ja Yu Dae Ryun Sae)

This is a variation of the back stance that is used during sparring. The feet are kept in the same placement as the back stance, but the weight is more evenly distributed (about 50-50). This means the front or back leg can be used equally. Chest and head face forward, with just the hips facing to the side. Hands are made into fists and arms are held in front of the body in a guarded position, ready to block or strike as needed.

Fighting Stance

T-Stance (Yup Sae)

The T-stance is a form of the back stance. To turn the back stance or fighting stance into a T-stance, slide the front foot forward and bend both knees to a 90-degree angle. This stance should look like a horse stance, except for the feet. Instead of both pointing ahead, parallel, they are perpendicular to each other. In sparring, sliding into a T-stance helps you to move into a different position or range more easily. By quickly sliding from the T-stance back into the back stance or the fighting stance, you can avoid any countering technique that your opponent makes.

Stance Secrets

In a front stance or a back stance, your forward leg is called your front leg and your back leg is called the rear or back leg. It is important to remember this because kicks that use the front leg are different from kicks that use the back leg. (In a horse stance, your front leg

The T-stance begins in a back stance. Slide the front leg forward, bending the knee to a 90-degree angle. The heels should be perpendicular to each other. Otherwise, the stance now resembles a horse stance.

is your left leg if you are looking to the left, your right leg if you are looking to the right, and neither leg if you are looking straight ahead.)

Practicing the various stances can be an excellent way to stretch. Try getting into each stance position and lowering your body as much as possible. Hold the stance stretch for 30 seconds. This gives a good stretch while helping you improve your stances.

A traditional method of building strength is to hold a stance for a very long period of time. Usually this is done by getting into the horse stance and lowering your body as far as you can, then holding it for three minutes, relaxing and repeating. Eventually, you can move to five minutes, then 10 minutes. This builds very strong quadriceps muscles and improves kicking techniques. You don't have to limit this strength building exercise to the horse stance. Any or all of the stances can be used.

This method of strength training is also an exercise used to lower your chi. "Lowering chi" is a method of creating a strong stance and at the same time trying to remain immovable. In addition to staying in a low horse stance for a long period of time, you can have a partner push at your shoulders, trying to knock you off balance. Your goal is to keep in the same position no matter what your partner does. If you work on this, then in sparring or in a confrontation, you will be strong enough to stay balanced and on your feet. This is extremely important because you never want to fall to the ground during sparring or an actual fight. "Going to the ground" means you will have to grapple, and it is extremely difficult to win this type of fight.

Stance Stepping and Turning

When practicing the martial arts, you'll need to move forward and back while maintaining your stance. You'll also need to be able to turn from one direction to another while remaining

Horse Stance Stretch
Assume a strong horse stance position (far left), bending knees deeply. Lean forward and sink lower into the stance (left). Hold the position for 15 seconds.

Front Stance Stretch
Assume a strong front stance (left). Bend forward leg as deeply as possible (right). Hold for 15 seconds.

Back Stance Stretch
Assume a back stance. Lower both knees until they're deeply bent. Hold for 15 seconds.

in your stance. This is necessary not only for practicing forms and fighting techniques, but for self-defense, in case you have more than one attacker. Stance stepping and turning are done differently for each stance.

Horse Stance Stepping

With the horse stance, any movement is usually to the side. In this case, you will simply slide one leg until it rests near the other, and then slide that leg until you are in another horse stance. Sometimes this technique is used in jumping kicks, in which case it is done quickly, without a noticeable stop. Sometimes you will go from a horse stance to a front stance. This is done by simply moving one leg forward until the other leg (your back leg) is straight and your front leg is bent at a 90-degree angle.

Horse Stance Turning

If you need to turn from one direction to another while in a horse stance, simply plant one foot and use it as a pivot point, moving the other foot forward or back, depending on what direction you wish to move.

Horse Stance Stepping
Assume a horse stance (left). Draw one leg into the other, for instance left leg into right leg (middle). Slide the other leg to the new horse stance position (right).

Front Stance Stepping

In front stance stepping, you simply step forward with your back leg. It becomes your front leg, bent at a 90-degree angle. What was your front leg now becomes your back leg, and is kept straight, with the heel resting on the ground. As you step forward, keep your knees bent so that you don't bounce up and down as you move. Your back foot should keep contact with the ground at all times. Slide your back foot up and in until it touches your front foot. Then slide it forward and out so that it becomes your front foot. Slid-

Front Stance Stepping
Assume a front stance (left). Slide the back leg forward and in so that it nearly touches the front leg. (middle). Clontinue sliding the back leg forward and out until it becomes the new front leg. (right).

Front Stance Turning
Assume a front stance (left). Turn and look in the new direction. Pick up your back leg and slide it outward, pivoting on your forward leg (middle). Plant your back leg forward in the new position. It is now the forward leg in the front stance, so the knee should be bent 90 degrees.

ing your foot toward your other foot protects your groin area as you move forward.

To move backward, simply reverse the sequence. The front leg slides back and in, then continues back and out until it becomes the back leg.

Front Stance Turning

To turn in a front stance, pick up your back leg, pivot 90 or 180 degrees on your front foot and place your back foot forward in the new direction. The back leg becomes the front leg in the new direction.

Back Stance Stepping
Assume a back stance (left). Step forward with the back leg. Pivot on the supporting foot (middle). Place the back leg in front, so that it becomes the forward foot. Your heels should remain at a 90-degree angle to each other (right).

Back Stance Turning

Assume a back stance (left). Turn your upper body to the new direction (middle). Redistribute weight so that most of it rests on the new back leg (right).

Back Stance Turning

From front...   *...to...*   *...back.*

Back Stance Stepping

Stepping with the back stance, the fighting stance and the T-stance is accomplished in the same way. Pick up your back leg, pivot on your supporting foot and place your back foot straight in front of you. Your back foot becomes your front foot. Your feet should move so that they remain perpendicular to each other in this new direction.

Back Stance Turning

To change direction in a back stance, merely turn your upper body from front to back. Shift your feet so that they remain perpendicular to each other in this new direction. Your front should face forward; your back foot should face the side. Redistribute your weight so that most of it rests on the new back foot.

Practice stance stepping and turning throughout your Tae Kwon Do workout so that it becomes second nature. Sometimes repeating the instructions to yourself out loud can help. (You'll hear lots of beginning and intermediate martial artists mumbling to themselves, "Pick up your back leg and turn...")

8

Basic Hand Striking Techniques *(Chigi)*

Hand striking techniques are those techniques that use any part of the hand as the striking surface. The striking surface is that part of your body that actually makes the impact. In fighting, hand techniques are used for close-range fighting, when kicks won't work.

When you practice fighting techniques, one tendency among beginning martial artists is favoring one hand or one leg. For example, if they're right-handed, they'll do all of their hand striking techniques with their right hand. This leads to a lack of balance.

You should be able to use both hands and both feet to strike, with equal skill. Always practice each technique for the same number of repetitions on each side. If you find a technique especially hard to do on one side, increase the number of repetitions you do on that side until you feel comfortable about the skill; then continue practicing an equal number of repetitions on each side.

Straight Punch *(Chung Kwon Chigi)*

The straight punch is the first hand technique the Tae Kwon Do student learns. To

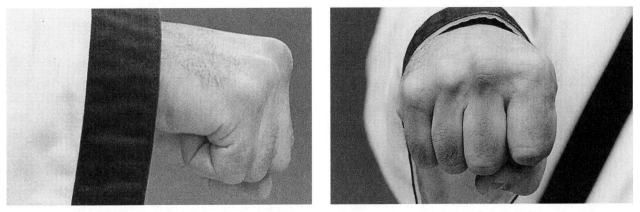

For a straight punch, make a fist by rolling your fingers into a ball and folding the thumb over (left). The wrist should remain straight and stable. The striking surface (right) for the straight punch is the first two knuckles of the fist.

49

begin, make a fist by rolling your fingers into a ball and folding your thumb over. The first two knuckles of your fist make up the striking area. Chamber your arm at your side by pulling your arm back and bending your elbow at a 90-degree angle. Your palm should be facing up. Punch forward with your arm. At the end of the strike, twist your wrist so that your palm faces down. This is done to add explosive power to the impact of your punch.

The punch extends from slightly above the waist forward, with the power of your shoulder and hips behind it. The two knuckles that make up the striking surface can strike to any target.

This technique is sometimes called *chireugi* or corkscrew punch since the wrist twists at the end to add power.

The straight punch moves from the side directly forward.

Reverse Punch

This is a variation of the straight punch. Since it generates more power, it is used almost exclusively. The reverse punch is performed in exactly the same way as the straight punch. The only difference is the placement of your feet. Remember, in a front stance or a back stance, your forward leg is called your front leg and the back leg is called the rear or back leg. If you punch with the hand that is on the same side as your front leg, you are throwing a straight punch. If you throw a punch from the same side as your back leg, it is called a reverse punch. Therefore, if your left leg is forward and you punch with your left hand, you are performing a straight punch. If your left leg is forward and you punch with your right hand, you are performing a reverse punch. You are usually able to generate more power with a reverse punch because of your body position. That is, you can pivot your hips into the punch to get the full force of your entire body behind it.

Punching Secrets

An important element of punching is to strike with the correct target area. This means that you must hold your wrist straight so that your knuckles are on the same plane as your forearm. The best way to ensure that you are striking with the first two knuckles of your fist is to use a striking post, which is simply an upright piece of wood, sometimes covered with carpet or other material to prevent cuts, that has been secured to the floor or the ground. If a striking post is not available, use any flat surface, such as a wall. Don't punch full power, of course, or you'll end up repairing the wall. Practice the punch slowly, extending your arm out until your fist touches the wall. Only the first two knuckles should make contact with the surface. Adjust your fist and the way you hold your hand and arm until you are striking with the correct striking surface.

Another problem is that martial artists have a tendency to roll their wrists. That is, they punch and their hand rolls so that their wrist bends. This can be dangerous, causing sprains

Reverse Punch

The back hand — striking hand — is chambered at the side, palm up, resting slightly above the waist (left). The punch travels directly to the target (middle). The wrist twists so that the palm faces down at the moment of impact (right).

Side view of the reverse punch.

or tears. For this reason, it is a good idea to practice punching a striking post or heavy bag to build the strength in your wrist so that this doesn't occur. You might invest in wrist wraps or bag gloves to keep your wrists steady until you've strengthened your wrist and arm muscles sufficiently. An old martial art trick for strengthening wrists is to do knuckle push-ups. These are done just like standard push-ups, but instead of placing palms a shoulder's width apart, the hands are made into fists and the push-up is done from this position.

Chamber and Twist

Two very important concepts to remember about punching are the chamber position and the wrist twist. The chamber position is the ready position of your hand and arm. Make sure your arm is cocked slightly above your waist

51

Wrist Twist
The punch starts with the palm up (left). The punch ends with the wrist twisted so that the palm faces down (right).

with a strong 90-degree angle. All Tae Kwon Do techniques have a starting position, called the chamber, that is essential to the correct performance of the technique. The twist is also extremely important; it helps generate explosive power at the point of impact. Almost all Tae Kwon Do hand and arm techniques, including strikes and blocks, require a twist at the end, so it is an important part of the technique to practice.

Punch/Pull

As you become more comfortable with the straight punch and the reverse punch, you can add elements to increase the power and effectiveness of your punches. Since Tae Kwon Do was influenced by the circular movements of Chinese martial arts, it is possible to incorporate a circular movement into your punching

to improve it. For instance, instead of simply punching forward with your punching hand, you can also pull back with your nonpunching hand. The best way to practice this is to get into a front stance and chamber both hands at your waist. Reach forward slightly with your back hand (which should be made into a fist); then, as you punch with your forward hand, pull your outstretched hand to your side, returning it to the chamber position with the palm up. Leave your front hand out in front. Punch forward with your back hand, pulling your front hand to your side as you do so. With some repetition, this will come naturally and will improve the power of your punches. It's also a skill that can be built on later. For instance, you may reach forward and grab your opponent with your back hand, pulling him or her toward you as you throw your punch forward. This increases the impact of the punch.

Punch/Pull

The punch/pull technique begins with the nonpunching arm forward in front of the body (left). As the punching hand moves forward, the nonpunching hand pulls back (middle). At impact, (right) the punching hand lands, while the nonpunching hand returns to chamber at the side, ready to punch.

Knife Hand Strike *(Sudo Chigi)*

A knife hand strike is a technique that uses the outer edge of your hand (the little finger edge) as the striking surface. The elbow is slightly bent and the hand open. Performed with fingers bent, it is called a "bear claw strike."

To make your hand into a knife hand, keep all your fingers and your thumb straight. Tighten your muscles so that there are no gaps between your fingers. Keep your wrist straight. The basic knife hand strike is executed by cocking your knife hand, palm up, near the opposite side shoulder. Then, strike across your body, straightening your elbow as you go. As you reach your target, twist your wrist so your palm faces down. This means you will have a sharper impact. The hand that you are not striking with should remain a fist at your side. By extending this fist slightly forward and then pulling it back

as you strike, you can create the punch (strike)/pull movement necessary for the correct execution of the technique.

45-Degree Knife Hand Strike

This is a simple variation of the knife hand strike. For this technique, you chamber your knife hand, palm up, near the same side shoulder. As you strike forward, extending your elbow, you tilt your hand to a 45-degree angle, so that your hand comes down on your target. Snap your wrist at impact to add power to the strike.

Ridge Hand Strike *(Yeop Sudo Chigi)*

The ridge hand strike uses the inner edge of your hand (the thumb edge) as the striking area. The strike is similar to the knife hand strike. To make a ridge hand, straighten your

Knife Hand Strike

Begin by chambering your hand in the knife hand position, palm up, near the opposite shoulder (left). Sweep your hand forward across your body (middle), the palm remaining upward (right).

At the moment of impact, the wrist is turned so that the palm faces down and the outer edge of the hand strikes the target.

(1)   (2)   (3)   (4)

45-Degree Knife Hand Strike
Chamber your hand in the knife hand position, palm up, above the same side shoulder (1).
Sweep forward with the knife hand (2). Slice down with the knife hand at a 45-degree angle (3).
Strike with the outer edge of the hand (4).

fingers. Fold your thumb under your hand so that the edge of your hand is smooth. Tighten your fingers so that there are no gaps. Start with your ridge hand extended out to the side, horizontal to the ground. Quickly sweep your arm across your body, pivoting at the waist and hips as you do so. Strike the target with the inner edge of your hand.

Ridge Hand Strike
Extend your arm horizontal to the ground, hand in a ridge hand position. Sweep arm forward (left). Keeping the arm horizontal and the elbow straight, continue sweeping toward the target (middle). Pivot at the waist and hips to add power at the moment of impact (right).

Reverse Ridge Hand Strike

Hold the hand in the ridge hand position, under the opposite arm, palm down (left, above). Sweep outsward with the ridge hand while pulling the nonstriking hand back (middle). Keep the elbow slightly bent as the strike sweeps outward (right, above). Twist the palm up at the moment of impact, striking with the inner edge of the hand (left below).

Ridge hand position from the side.

Reverse Ridge Hand Strike

This is a variation of the ridge hand strike. With your ridge hand held under the opposite arm, palm down, swing your arm outward toward your target, moving across your body. Keep your elbow slightly bent. At the moment of impact, twist your wrist so that your palm faces up. Strike with the thumb edge of your hand.

Palm Strike *(Chang Kwon Chigi)*

This technique can be used in place of the punch and is executed in nearly the same way. The difference is in the striking surface. The heel of the palm is used instead of the knuckles. Instead of making your hand into a fist, make it into a knife hand. Chamber your hand near your waist, with fingers pointing down and palm facing forward. Pull your fingers

Palm Strike
The palm is chambered at the waist, hand in the palm strike position, fingers pointing down (left, above). The hand moves directly forward from the body, traveling straight to the target (middle). As the palm strikes the target, twist the wrist so that the fingers point up (right, above). Bottom right, side view of a palm strike.

Reverse Palm Strike

With the nonstriking hand in front to give a balanced pulling motion, the back hand is held chambered at the side in the palm strike position (left). As the reverse palm strike moves forward, the nonstriking hand is pulled back (middle). As the reverse palm strike lands, twist the wrist so that the fingers point up. The nonstriking hand is returned to the chamber position, ready to strike (right).

The palm strike in action.

back so that the heel of your hand is slightly more forward and will strike the target first. Tighten your hand so that there are no gaps. Strike forward with your hand, twisting your wrist at the moment of impact so that your fingers point up, but the heel of the hand is still forward.

Reverse Palm Strike

This is a variation of the palm strike. Instead of striking with the hand on the same side as the forward leg, you will strike with the hand on the same side as the back leg.

Hand Striking Secrets

For all hand striking techniques, chambering, twisting and pulling with the opposite hand all increase the power and effectiveness of your techniques. Once you've learned the techniques themselves, you can generate more power by following these ideas:

Use Your Body

Most new martial artists make the mistake of only using their arms to generate power in their hand striking techniques. They do this by throwing only the arm forward. A similar problem is when martial artists overextend their arms. This usually happens when you try to add power to a punch or striking technique by throwing your arm so that your shoulder rolls forward. Regardless of technique, your shoulder should always stay on the same plane as your chest. Don't let your shoulder roll forward beyond your chest.

To generate more power, you need to put your whole body behind your strike, not just your arm. This is done by using your hips to move your body back and forth. To understand how this works, stand in a front stance. Chamber your fist at your side. As you punch forward, twist the same side hip forward as well. You should notice a sizeable difference in the power of your strikes. You can also step or slide into a punch or other hand strike to add power. Practice this by stepping forward and striking at the same time. Combine the step and the hip pivot at the same time to really increase the power of your hand strikes.

Use a Punching Bag

It's difficult to measure the power of your hand striking techniques without using a punching bag or other target. Use bag gloves or sparring equipment, especially if you haven't been doing much bag work. Try the body techniques listed above on the heavy bag to see how they improve your hand striking techniques. To get the most from these suggestions, practice for several minutes on the heavy bag each day. Remember to try other hand techniques, like the knife hand, ridge hand and palm strike. Also, try varying your footwork so that sometimes you are in a front stance, sometimes a back stance or fighting stance, and sometimes a horse stance.

Improve Upper Body Strength

One key to explosive power in your hand striking techniques is to build your upper body strength. Although you can certainly lift weights to become stronger, nothing quite compares to the old-fashioned push-up for strengthening your upper arms and chest muscles. Start with the very basic ones and build up from there.

Lie flat on the floor and place your palms on the floor directly under your shoulders, about a shoulder's width apart. Keeping your abdomen tight and your back and shoulders straight, push up. If these are difficult to do at first, rest your knees on the floor. Start with three sets of 15 push-ups each, progressing to five sets of 15 push-ups each. Your goal is to be able to do 75 push-ups, resting only your palms and toes on the floor. You can vary the push-ups and their effects on your body by changing the placement of your hands. You can spread your hands so they are extended two shoulders' widths apart. You can bring your hands in close under your sternum to work your triceps. Finally, you can work on that martial artist's standby, the knuckle push-up. These are done by making your hands into fists and resting your weight on the first two knuckles of each hand (your punching knuckles). Knuckle push-ups strengthen your wrists so that they won't roll when you punch.

If a pull-up bar (sometimes called a chin-up) is available, work on pull-ups. If you can't do these well at first, don't give up. Have a friend act as a spotter at first. Grip the bar with hands about a shoulder's width apart and pull straight up. Don't overstrain. You can vary the pull-up by changing the grip you have on the bar. Aim to do three sets of three pull-ups without a spotter's help. Once you can do these easily, increase by increments of three. Your upper body strength will have increased considerably by the time you can do 25 pull-ups.

Main Key to Successful Hand Strikes

Because there are so many elements of a good hand striking technique, sometimes you can spend too much time worrying about perfect execution. Then when you go to strike, you do so tentatively, feeling unsure whether you are doing the technique correctly. So the key is to always strike with confidence. It may not be a perfect punch, and you may not get your hips pivoted exactly right, but if you have confidence behind your techniques, you'll always be a step ahead of everyone else.

9

Intermediate Hand Striking Techniques *(Chigi)*

Once you understand how the basic hand strikes work, you can move onto the intermediate techniques.

Spear Hand Strike *(Kwansu)*

The spear hand technique, sometimes called spear fingers, is performed in a way similar to the straight punch. Put your hand into the knife hand position. Fingers should be straight and your muscles should be tight so that there are no gaps between fingers. The tips of the fingers are held even with each other. You can bend your thumb at the knuckle to help strengthen the spear hand position. For the spear hand,

Spear Hand Strike
Hand is held in the chamber position, palm up, near the waist (left). Spear hand travels directly forward (middle). As the hand lands, turn the wrist over so that the palm faces down (right).

the striking surface is the tips of your fingers, so you'll need to keep your fingers "strong" — that is, you must make sure your fingers won't bend under impact. One way to practice this is to strike the open palm of your other hand with your spear hand until you are comfortable with the position and strength of your fingers.

With your fingers in the spear hand position, chamber your hand palm up near your waist. Your opposite hand should be a fist. Strike straight forward with your hand, turning your palm down at the moment of impact. The tips of your fingers should thrust into your target.

Spear hand strike from the side.

Spear hand in the throat grab position.

Spear Hand Throat Grab

The spear hand strike can be used as a throat grab by modifying the spear hand position. The thumb is moved away from the fingers, resulting in a V-shaped hand. The strike is thrown forward toward the opponent's throat.

Spear hand throat grab in action.

Two-Finger Strike

The hand is held in the two-finger strike position, palm up, chambered at the waist (above, left). The strike travels directly forward (middle). As the strike lands, twist the wrist so that the palm faces down (above, right). At left is a side view of the two-finger strike, while at bottom left is a close-up view of the two-finger strike position. Below, the eyes are the target of the two-finger strike.

Two-Finger Strike

This technique is a variation of the spear hand. With your fingers in a spear hand position, fold your two smallest fingers down and hold them in place with your thumb. Bend your forefinger and index finger to an angle that's not quite 90 degrees. With your hand chambered at your side, palm up, strike forward. Turn your wrist so that your palm faces down at the moment of impact. Your target area is your opponent's eyes, so this strike always moves upward.

Back Fist Strike *(Choo Muk Dung Chigi)*

This technique makes use of the back of the fist as the striking surface. This technique is also usually reserved for the opponent's head (thus its alternative name, "temple strike"). Therefore, it is directed at a high area.

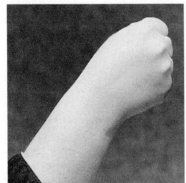

Back Fist hand position

The back fist is executed by making a fist with your hand. Chamber your fist near the opposite shoulder, with the palm facing outward. Sweep outward from your body, twisting your wrist at the moment of impact so that the back of your fist strikes the target area.

Hammer Fist Strike
(Choomuk-Pahdak Chigi)

The hammer fist, also called bottom fist, is a simple technique, although it is not taught until the intermediate stage of Tae Kwon Do training. The hand is made into a fist. The bottom of the hand is the striking surface. Chamber your hammer fist above the same side shoulder, with the bottom of your hand facing up and out. Then, in a circular motion, make an arc so that the bottom of your fist strikes the target. This downward strike is only used when striking from above a target area. The key to an effective hammer fist strike is to use a circular motion, which generates speed and power.

Horizontal Hammer Fist Strike

A variation of the hammer fist strike is the horizontal hammer fist strike. This begins chambered at the opposite shoulder and sweeps outward across the body.

Back Fist Strike
The back fist is held chambered near the opposite shoulder, palm facing out (left). Sweep the fist outward from the body (middle). As the strike lands, twist so that the palm faces inward (right).

Hammer Fist Strike
The hammer fist is held above the same-side shoulder, with the bottom of the fist facing up and out (left). Swing the fist down in an arc (middle). The strike lands directly on the target (right).

*Horizontal
Hammer Fist Strike*
Chamber the hammer fist near the opposite shoulder (right). Sweep out from the body, keeping the fist horizontal to the floor and striking the target from the side (far right).

Backward Hammer Fist Strike
The hammer fist is chambered near the same-side shoulder (left). The hand is swept down. Turn your head to see the target behind you (middle). Strike with the bottom of the hammer fist, aiming for the target to the rear of you (right).

Backward Hammer Fist Strike

A variation of this technique is to use the hammer fist to strike to the back. For this, the hammer fist is chambered near the same side shoulder, the bottom of the fist facing upward. By striking downward and extending the elbow, you can strike a target behind you at hip level. This techniques works well to strike to the groin. To make this a more powerful technique, turn your shoulder and upper body into it.

Hammer Fist Position

Secrets of Boxing

Although most martial arts schools don't teach the techniques of boxing, they are good skills to have, and will add considerably to your repertoire of martial arts techniques. You can practice these techniques on a heavy bag or practice them in a shadow workout. Adding some boxing drills will make your workouts more interesting and more productive. Understanding and practicing these techniques will make your other hand striking techniques better and more powerful. And, since you might run into these techniques outside the training hall, they're good to know.

Boxing Stance

Boxing techniques begin with a modified fighting stance. This is done by keeping one foot more forward than the other, as in a fighting stance. Both your feet and your body should face the target. Your back shoulder should be turned

The boxing stance is a modified fighting stance. The entire body faces forward, one foot slightly ahead of the other. The opposite shoulder is turned slightly away. Hands, made into fists, guard the face at all times. Elbows are kept tucked to protect the ribs.

ers have right-hand jabs.) But since martial arts emphasize balance, you'll need to always work both sides of your body equally. Therefore, practice both right- and left-hand jabs.

The jab is done with the hand that is on the same side as the forward foot. Instead of chambering your fist at the waist, as you do for martial arts punches, your jabbing fist should protect your jaw until you are ready to use it. Then, punch forward from your jaw, extending your elbow. Turn your body so that your shoulder goes into the punch as well. Pivot on your forward foot so that instead of pointing at your target, your toes are perpendicular to it at the time of impact.

Cross

Once you understand the way a jab works, you're ready to add the cross. The cross is usually done with the stronger arm, but be sure to practice with both to make your martial arts practice balanced. The cross is performed with the arm on the same side as the back leg. It almost invariably follows the jab. Your fist should be protecting your jaw. Drop your hand slightly so that your fist is facing your target. Punch forward, extending your elbow while turning your upper body into the blow. Both feet should pivot in the direction of the punch to add power.

Hook

The hook is usually performed on the same side as the jab; that is, on the same side as the forward foot. However, it can also be executed using the back hand. The hook is done by cocking the arm at the elbow at close to a 90-degree angle. The cocked arm should be horizontal to the floor. Pivot on your feet in the direction of the punch. Your arm should remain cocked as you swing your body forward. The best way to understand this is to think of leading with your shoulder. Your shoulder should turn toward the target with your cocked arm following. At no point do you extend your elbow. As you turn your body, your arm will hook or arc slightly forward, striking the target as you pivot.

slightly away to make you a smaller target, and for generating more power when you punch with that hand. You'll want to stay light on your feet, since you'll be pivoting frequently to make the most of your body power. Your hands should always be made into fists. They should be held one on each side of your jaw. This protects you from those knockout punches. Even when you begin punching, one hand should remain up to protect your jaw at all times. Tuck your elbows in to protect your ribs from body blows.

Jab

The jab is a technique that is not necessarily intended to knock out the opponent. It is usually used to feel out the opponent's strengths and weaknesses, to see how the opponent will react to your punches. It can also be used to distract him or her. You might jab to the body to lower your opponent's guard, and then quickly follow with another technique to the head, which will be unguarded.

Usually, boxers jab with their left hand, because they are right-handed and they like to follow a jab with a stronger technique using their stronger arm. (Obviously, left-handed box-

Jab

Assume a boxing stance, one leg slightly forward (left, above). Punch directly forward with the front hand. Don't drop the punch (right, above). Pivot the hips as you throw the punch. The target is the head (right).

Cross

From the boxing stance, the back hand is thrown forward (left). Pivot the hips into the punch as your hand comes across your body (right). The punch can be aimed at the head or the body.

Hook

Since the hook usually follows the cross, the body is pivoted slightly away from the target (left). The arm, cocked at about a 90-degree angle, is held horizontal to the floor. Pivot the hips and turn the shoulder into the punch (middle). The arm, elbow still cocked, connects with the target (right).

Uppercut
Keeping the forward hand up to protect the head, drop your back hand down and slightly behind (top left). Pivot into the punch as you bring your arm upward (top right). Extend the punching arm slightly into the target, punching with the top of the knuckles (bottom left). Continue to pivot into the uppercut to add power (bottom right).

Uppercut

In Tae Kwon Do, a punch similar to the uppercut is the upset punch. It can be performed with both hands at the same time. When done this way, it is called a double upset punch. The upset punch is an advanced Tae Kwon Do technique, however, so it isn't used by beginning or intermediate students.

The uppercut used in boxing is usually performed on the same side as the cross; that is, the same side as the back leg. The uppercut is a circular movement that strikes the target from underneath. It is done by keeping the fist near the jaw until you're ready to punch. Then, reach slightly behind and drop your arm to waist level. Pivot into the punch. Extend your arm forward and up, striking the target with the top of your knuckles.

Boxing Drills

In order to perform these techniques well, you need to practice them individually and then put them together into punching combinations. Once you understand how each technique works individually, try stringing several together.

Timing

In boxing, it is essential to work on timing, which is the ability to feint and punch while avoiding blows. To practice putting boxing techniques together, start simple. Do several jabs in a row as if you were feeling out an opponent. Then suddenly add a cross. Repeat this combination several times. Once you have the rhythm of the jab-punch combination, add the hook. Once you have the rhythm of the jab-punch-hook combination, add the uppercut. When do-

(1) (2) (3) (4)

Timing

Add techniques together to improve timing. Make several punches flow smoothly by practicing punch combinations. Begin in a good boxing stance (1). Next, throw a jab with your forward arm (2). Then bring your forward arm back to guard your chin (3). Throw a cross with the back hand (4).

(5) (6) (7) (8)

Next, cock the elbow of your forward arm in preparation for a hook (5). Strike with the hook (6). Bring the hooking hand back to protect the chin. Begin an uppercut with the back hand (7). Strike with the uppercut (8).

ing combinations, remember to bring the punching hand back to the jaw. One hand should be up, protecting the jaw, at all times.

Speed

In order to improve speed, which improves power, challenge yourself. Land a punch and pull it back quickly. Think of getting your fist back to protect your jaw as fast as possible. Once you can do this pretty quickly, add a twist by trying to land the next punch before your first punch is all the way back to your jaw. Try to increase the number of punches you can do this way without stopping.

Bob-and-Weave

Keep in mind that boxers have to remain light on their feet, not only so they can pivot into their punches, but so they can avoid their opponent's punches. One way to work on this is to dance around a heavy bag, or simply move around in a small circle, keeping your feet in motion all the time, stopping only now and then to throw a punch. You can also practice the boxer's bob-and-weave by circling and ducking. A partner can help by sweeping a hand target (or just a hand) in the direction of your jaw. Your goal is to duck and evade the hand.

Bob-and-Weave
Practice the bob-and-weave with a partner. Begin in a good boxing stance (top left). Have your partner sweep toward your head with a focus mitt or hand. Duck under the sweep (top right). When the target has swept past, step into position to punch (right).

10

Basic Blocks *(Maki)*

Blocking techniques are used to keep a hand technique or kick from landing on your body. By using stronger parts of your body to protect weaker parts, you'll be more likely to succeed in a confrontation. Also, blocked kicks and punches don't score points in freestyle sparring.

Different blocks are used depending on the area you are protecting. Low blocks protect your legs, especially your knees, which are extremely vulnerable. Middle blocks protect your midsection, such as your solar plexus and your ribs. High blocks protect your head and shoulders.

Low Block *(Hadan Maki)*

This is the first block a beginning Tae Kwon Do student learns. It is used to deflect punches and kicks delivered to the middle or low section, using the inner surface of the arm as the blocking surface. To perform a low block, stand in a front stance. With the arm that is on the same side as your forward leg, make a fist. Bring your arm up to your opposite shoulder, so that your palm faces up toward the ceiling. With a sweeping motion, bring your arm down across your body, turning your wrist so that your palm faces the outside. Your arm should stop slightly beyond your knee. The blocking surface for this technique is the fleshy part of

the arm. Keep your wrist and hand strong in case this part of your body comes in contact with the kick or hand strike that you are blocking.

High Block *(Sangdan Maki)*

The high block is an upward block that is used to protect the head and shoulders. It is done with the arm on the same side as the front leg. Place your opposite arm in front of your body. Both hands should be fists. Bend the blocking arm so that the fist is under your opposite arm, near the shoulder. Your palm faces down. Pulling your opposite arm back toward your side, sweep your blocking arm up, keeping your elbow cocked at a 45-degree angle. Your blocking arm should rise slightly above the top of your head. Twist your arm so that the palm of your hand and the fleshy side of your arm face the ceiling. You should be able to see under your block, and it should protect the top of your head from a downward strike.

Crescent Blocks *(Jungdan Maki)*

These blocks protect the middle section of your body, including your ribs and your solar plexus. They are performed by making a sweep-

Low Block

Assume a front stance. Chamber the fist of the blocking arm up near the opposite shoulder, palm facing up (left). Sweep the blocking arm down across the body (middle). Turn the wrist so that the palm faces down. The block should strike past the forward knee.

High Block

Bend your blocking arm under the opposite arm, palm facing up (left). Sweep the blocking arm upward (middle). Pull the nonblocking arm back to the chamber position. Your blocking arm should rise slightly above your head, the wrist twisting so that the palm faces outward (right).

Inside-Outside Crescent Block
In a back stance, chamber the forward arm by placing it under the opposite arm, palm facing down (Left). Sweep the forward arm toward the front leg (middle). The forearm of the blocking arm should rise until it is perpendicular to the floor. As the arm blocks, twist the wrist so that the palm faces in. Your elbow should be cocked at a 90-degree angle.

ing motion in front of your body. There are two kinds of crescent blocks: inside-outside blocks and outside-inside blocks. They are usually performed in a back stance.

Inside-Outside Block

The block is done with your forward arm. The back arm is cocked at the elbow, hand as a fist. Your blocking arm, hand as a fist, starts under your opposite arm, as with a high block. Your palm faces down and your arm is horizontal to the floor. Sweep your blocking arm out from your body so that it moves toward your forward leg. As it sweeps, your forearm should rise so that it is perpendicular to the ground. The elbow should be bent at a 90-degree angle. Pull your opposite (nonblocking) arm back to your side, chambering your fist with the palm up. This will prepare you to punch or to execute

another block. As your blocking arm crosses your forward leg, twist your forearm so that your palm faces you. This twist helps knock away the opponent's strike. Remember to keep your shoulder facing your target and your body facing away so that you are less vulnerable to a strike.

Outside-Inside Block

This block is also done with the forward arm. Again, both hands are fists. Instead of crossing the body, however, you will reach behind with your arm, twisting at the waist. Your elbow should be cocked so that your upper arm is horizontal to the floor and your forearm is perpendicular to it. Your palm faces forward. Your opposite arm, hand as a fist, is in front of your body. As you sweep with the blocking arm from back to front, pull your opposite arm back so

Outside-Inside Crescent Block
Reach behind with the forward arm, twisting at the waist. The elbow should be cocked at a 90-degree angle. The palm faces outward (left). Sweep your blocking arm from back to front, untwisting at the waist as you block. Pull your nonblocking arm back to the chamber position (middle). As the block lands slightly past the forward knee, twist your wrist so that the palm faces inward (right).

that it rests chambered at your waist, palm up and ready to strike or block. Untwist or uncoil at the waist as you sweep with the blocking arm. This explosive movement adds power to your block. As your block sweeps across your forward leg, twist your wrist so that your palm faces you.

Single Knife Hand Block (Sudo Maki)

The single knife hand block is performed in either a front or a back stance, and uses an open hand in the knife hand position. This block is used to prevent a strike to either the middle or the high area of your body. The blocking hand is the forward hand. Make your blocking hand into a knife hand by straightening the fingers and thumb and tightening the muscles. Your

back hand should be a fist; this arm should be extended in front of your body. The knife hand starts palm up between your opposite shoulder and your ear. Sweep your arm across your body, keeping your elbow cocked at a 90-degree angle. As your block reaches the front of your body, twist your wrist so the edge of your hand blocks, palm facing away from you. As you block, pull your opposite arm to your side, where it should stay in a chambered position, palm facing up.

Double Knife Hand Blocks

These are a variation of the single knife hand block. They use your nonblocking hand to protect your midsection. A double knife hand block can be used to block the middle

Single Knife Hand Block
Your forward hand is held chambered in a knife hand position near the opposite shoulder, palm facing inward (left). Sweep across your body, keeping the elbow at a 90-degree angle (middle). The block lands in line with the forward knee. As it lands, twist your wrist so that the palm faces outward. Your opposite arm should be pulled back and chambered at the side as the block is performed (right).

section or the low section; you will use a different blocking technique depending on whether you are blocking the middle section or the low section.

Double Knife Hand Block, Middle Section

Although this technique can be done in any stance, begin practicing it in a back stance. Both hands should be in a knife hand position. Reaching behind you, extend your arms straight back. As you reach, your forward arm should be across your chest, palm facing up. Your back arm should stretch far back behind you, palm down. Sweeping quickly, move your arms across your body so that your forward arm stops above your forward leg and your back arm covers your solar plexus. The elbow on your front blocking arm should remain cocked at a 90-degree angle. By twisting your wrists at the end of the block, more force is added. This means the palm of your forward arm should be facing out, away from your body, at the end of the block. You should be able to see over the tops of your fingers. Your back arm should come across your midsection, stopping in front of your body to protect your ribs and abdomen. This elbow should be bent at a 90-degree angle, and the palm should twist so that it faces up. Hold this arm slightly away from your body, keeping it strong so that any strike to that area won't drive your arm into your midsection.

Double Knife Hand Block, Middle Section
Reach straight back with both hands in the knife hand position. The forward hand should cross your chest, palm up, and your back hand should extend back, elbow straight, palm facing down (left). Sweep both arms quickly toward the front (middle). As the block lands, your forward hand should be in line with your forward leg. The wrist twists at the end so that the palm faces outward. Your elbow should be cocked at a 90-degree angle. Your back arm should come across your midsection as a guard. The wrist should twist so that the palm faces up (right).

Double Knife Hand Block, Low Section

This technique is performed in the same way as the double knife hand block to the middle section, with two variations. First, instead of reaching straight behind with both hands, you will reach behind and up so that your hands will move down in a direct line. Reach for the ceiling, hands in the same position as for the double knife hand block, middle section. This means your forward arm should come across your body, palm facing up. Your back arm should extend up as far as possible, palm facing down. As you block, your back hand will move to cover your midsection, twisting so that the palm faces up. Your forward arm blocks downward so that it is parallel to your front leg and 8 to 10 inches away from your leg. The palm should face your knee.

Double Knife Hand Block, Low Section

Reach back and up with both hands in the knife hand position. The forward hand should be across the chest, palm up. The back hand should extend behind you, reaching up. The elbow should be straight and the palm should be facing down (left). Sweep arms directly downward (middle). As the block lands, the forward hand should be parallel to the forward knee, fingers pointing toward the ground. Twist your wrist at the end of the block so that the palm faces the knee. Your back arm should come across your midsection as a guard. The wrist should twist so that the palm faces up.

11

Intermediate Blocks *(Maki)*

Intermediate blocks are slightly more sophisticated and are used in more complex situations than basic blocks are. Once you understand the workings of the basic blocks, you can begin practicing the intermediate blocks.

Single Forearm Block *(Pahl Maki)*

This block protects your middle section, and is similar to a crescent block. It is usually performed by standing in a back stance, both hands as fists. The forward arm does the blocking. The back arm should be extended slightly in front of your body. Your forward arm should rest on the opposite shoulder, palm facing up. Sweep across your body with your blocking arm, keeping the elbow cocked at a 90-degree angle. As you sweep, pull the opposite arm back to chamber at your waist. As your forward arm blocks, twist your wrist so that your palm faces away from your body. The fleshy part of your arm is the blocking surface.

Double Forearm Block *(Yang Pahl Maki)*

This is a variation of the single forearm block. In the double forearm block, one arm performs the actual block while the other aug-

ments the block, providing support and an additional guard. It can be performed as an inside-to-outside movement or an outside-to-inside movement.

In a front stance, both hands as fists, reach behind you with both arms. Your forward arm should be across your body, palm facing down. Your back arm should reach behind, palm down. Both arms should move at the same time as you block. Sweep your front arm out from your body so that it stops over your front leg. Twist

A side view of the double forearm block.

81

Single Forearm Block

Chamber the forward arm, hand as a fist, near the opposite shoulder, palm facing up (left). Sweep the forward arm out, pulling your opposite arm back to the chamber position (middle). As the forearm blocks in line with the forward knee, twist the wrist so that the palm faces away (right).

Double Forearm Block

Reach directly back with both arms, hands in fists. Both palms should face down (left). Sweep both arms across the body (middle). The forward arm should block in line with the forward knee. Your elbow should be cocked at a 90-degree angle. Twist your wrist as you block so that the palm faces in. Your back arm should augment the block, coming across the front of the body, fist resting against the side of the forward arm. The wrist should twist so that the palm faces up (right).

C-Block

Both hands are chambered at the waist. The forward hand is chambered above the back hand. Both hands are fists and both palms face up (left). Both arms block simultaneously. Your forward hand sweeps across the body and the back hand rises above your head (middle). The forward arm blocks above the forward knee. The wrist twists so that the palm faces out, as in a forearm block. The back arm blocks above the head, wrist twisting so that the palm faces out (right).

your wrist so that your palm faces up. Bring your back arm across your body, twisting your wrist so that the palm faces up. The fist from your back arm should rest on the side of your front forearm, protecting your midsection. Your front arm and back arm should form a 90-degree angle in front of your body.

C-Block

The c-block is so named because your arms make the shape of a "C." This block protects both the middle and high sections. Basically, it is a high block and a forearm block performed simultaneously. It is usually done in a back stance. Both hands are made into fists and both hands rest above the hip of the back leg. Both palms face up. The back hand rests below the front hand. Both hands move at the same time when you are ready to block. The forward hand

sweeps across the middle section of your body and stops at the front leg. Twist your wrist as you block so that your palm and the fleshy part of your arm face away from your body. Keep your elbow cocked at a 90-degree angle. You should be able to see above your block. At the same time, your back arm rises above your head. Your wrist twists outward so that your palm and the fleshy part of your arm face away from your body. Your arm should be a few inches above and away from the top of your head. Your elbow should remain cocked at a 90-degree angle.

Open Hand C-Block

A variation of the c-block is the open hand c-block. It is executed in exactly the same way with this exception: both hands are held in the shape of a knife hand.

Open Hand C-Block
Chamber your hands as for a c-block, except hands should be in a knife hand position (left). As in the regular c-block, the forward arm sweeps across the body and the back arm rises to block high (middle). Both wrists twist so that the palms face out (right).

Spear Block
Extend the back arm straight back. The hand should be a fist and the palm should be facing down (left). Bring the arm forward, pivoting your hip forward at the same time (middle). Complete the block by twisting your arm upward. Your palm should face inward. The hip should pivot so that your chest faces the side (right).

Spear Block (Doll Rye Maki)

This technique was used in ancient times to protect the martial artist's body from a spear thrust. It can be used to deflect many types of kicks. It is usually performed in a front stance. Again, both hands are fists. In this block, your back arm does the blocking. Your forward arm is extended slightly in front of you, and as you perform the block, you will pull it (the non-blocking arm) back to its chamber position at your side. To execute the spear block, swing your back arm in an arc behind you, keeping your elbow at a 90-degree angle. Then, bring your arm forward, twisting upward and outward, keeping your elbow cocked. Pivot your body so that your hips turn away from the blocking arm. Although there are several different steps, they should be performed smoothly without stopping. The goal is to move the weapon (or kick) away from your body without trying to stop it with a direct block. As you block, pivot on both feet so that your shoulder and hip face forward. This presents a narrower target for your opponent. At the end of the block, your palm should be facing to the side, and you should be twisted at the waist to present your hip and shoulder.

Blocking Secrets

The most important thing to remember about blocks is to execute them quickly and sharply. The momentum will help you defend against an attack. Your blocks should be as powerful as your kicks and punches are.

In most cases, you will be blocking with the most muscular (fleshy) part of your arm. If you were to block with the back of your forearm, for example, the force of blocking an attack could break your arm. Therefore, it is important to perform the wrist or arm twist that is described for each block.

Different blocks are used to block and protect different areas. To sharpen your skills, ask a partner to strike at any section of your body; you respond with a block appropriate to that section. If you don't have a partner, call out target areas (i.e., "head" or "knee") at random and then execute an appropriate block.

The blocking surface of the arm for most blocks.

12

Basic Kicking Techniques
(Chaki)

Kicking techniques are those techniques that use any part of the foot as the striking surface. Like punches, they are best used from a certain range. Kicks are most effective when the opponent is several feet away. Hand striking techniques are more effective when the opponent is closer.

Some kicking techniques can be performed with either the front or back leg. For instance, if you are in a front stance, you can do a front kick with your forward leg or with your back leg. The only difference is how you shift your weight. A front leg front kick requires you to move your weight to the back leg as you kick, whereas a back leg front kick requires you to move your weight to the front leg. (The "front" in "front kick" refers to the location of the target — in front of you — not the leg you use to make the kick). Although front and back leg kicks are basically executed in the same way, they have different purposes. The front leg kick is always a faster kick than the back leg kick, but the back leg kick is always more powerful than the front leg kick. Therefore, which you use will depend on circumstances. The faster kick might distract an opponent whereas the more powerful kick might disable him or her.

As you learn more about Tae Kwon Do, especially sparring, it will become easier to judge when to use which kick. You will find that some kicks suit your abilities better than others, but all kicks should be practiced, since each helps you improve certain aspects of your martial arts training.

Front Kick *(Ap Chaki)*

This kick is used for a target directly in front of you. It can be used to strike a low, middle or high target area. The striking surface is the ball of your foot. To arrive at this position, point your foot and pull your toes back. To perform the kick, lift your leg high, bending your knee to a 90 degree angle. Your leg should be slightly in front of your body. Snap your leg forward, striking with the ball of your foot.

The front kick can emphasize different motions. The snap front kick is performed with a sharp whipping movement and has the advantage of speed. The push or thrust front kick is performed by pushing the target away with the foot. This kick can use the whole foot. Its advantage is power. The instep front kick is a front kick that uses the instep as the striking surface. It is used to kick upward into the groin.

Front Leg Front Kick

Assume a front stance (left). Chamber the front leg by lifting the leg high and bending the knee to a 90-degree angle. Point your foot and pull your toes back (middle). Snap your leg forward, striking with the ball of the foot (right).

Back Leg Front Kick

Assume a front stance (left). Chamber the back leg by lifting it high and bending the knee 90 degrees (middle). Strike directly forward with the ball of the foot (right).

*Side Views of the Front Kick
Front kick to the low section
(above left). Front kick to the
middle section (above right). Front
kick to the high section (right).*

Crescent Kicks
(Chiki Chaki)

These kicks are circular kicks. The striking surface is either the inner or the outer edge of the foot, depending on what direction the kick is coming from. There are two kinds of crescent kicks: inside-outside (uses the outer edge) and outside-inside (uses the inner edge). There is also a variation, called an axe kick, which uses the heel.

In a crescent kick, the kicking leg travels in an arc, moving across the body. The leg is swung up as high as possible, then brought down quickly.

Inside-Outside Crescent Kick

In a front stance, lift your back leg from the ground. Sweep it forward, coming slightly across your body, and swinging your leg as far upward as you can. Continue the kick by sweeping to the side in a circular movement. This is

(1)

(3)

**Inside-Outside
Crescent Kick**
*Assume a short front stance
(1). Lift your back leg (2).
Swing the back leg up in an
arc, moving it from the inside
to the outside (3). Strike with
the outer edge of the foot at
the top of the arc (4). Return
to the starting position (5).*

(2)

(4)

(5)

the actual strike. The outer edge of the foot is the striking surface, and should be used to strike a high target area (shoulder or head, for instance.) Finish the kick by landing with your foot in the same position it started from.

Outside-Inside Crescent Kick

This is the same type of kick, only it travels in the opposite direction. In a front stance, lift your back leg from the ground. Sweep to the side, bringing your leg as high up as possible.

(1)

(2)

(3)

(4)

(5)

Outside-Inside Crescent Kick
Assume a short front stance (1). Lift your back leg (2). Swing the leg up in an arc, moving from the outside to the inside, striking with the inner edge of the foot (3). Return to the starting position (4 and 5).

Pull your leg slightly across your body. This is the actual strike. The inner edge of the foot is the striking surface. The target area should be high. Finish by landing with your foot in the same position it started from.

Axe Kick

The axe kick is a crescent kick, slightly modified for more power. It can be performed either outside-inside or inside-outside. The only difference is the direction of the kick. In an axe

91

kick, the striking surface is the heel of the foot. As the crescent kick reaches the top of its arc, either moving toward the body (outside-inside crescent kick) or away from the body (inside-outside crescent kick), pull your leg downward sharply and quickly, striking the top of the target with the back of your heel. Then return your foot to its starting position.

Side Kick *(Yup Chaki)*

The side kick uses the bottom of your heel and the knife edge of your foot to strike. The leg is drawn up (chambered) and then thrust out as the supporting foot pivots. The side kick can be performed in any stance, but to learn the technique, begin by assuming a front stance position. Your target area is directly in front of you.

Lift your back leg up high, pivoting on your supporting foot and pulling your kicking leg up high. Cock your knee so that it is bent at least 90 degrees. Keep your foot tight by making it parallel to the floor. This is the chamber position. Continue to pivot on your supporting foot. You should pivot 180 degrees, so that the toes of your supporting foot point away from the target. Snap your kicking leg out, extending your knee. Lean slightly over your supporting leg to maintain your balance. Strike your target with the heel of your foot. The toes of your striking foot should be at least parallel to the floor. If possible, they should be turned slightly toward the floor. This helps you strike your target correctly. Never strike with your toes pointing upward, as this can injure your foot and is poor technique.

Jump Side Kick *(Eidan Yup Chaki)*

This is a variation of the side kick that includes a jump. A slide or step can be used instead of the jump; such a kick is used for covering ground without losing your balance. To perform a jump side kick, stand in a horse stance. Move your supporting leg in so that it almost touches the foot of your kicking leg. Chamber your kicking leg by picking it up high and cocking the knee 90 degrees. Kick straight out to the side. No pivoting or turning is necessary. As you become more proficient with the tech-

Side Kick
Assume a front stance (left). Chamber the kicking leg by lifiting the leg high and cocking the knee to a 90-degree angle. The foot is held tight, at a 90-degree angle to the shin. As the leg is chambered, the supporting foot pivots 90 degrees (middle). Snap the kicking leg out, striking with the heel of the foot. The knee is straightened and the supporting foot pivots another 90 degrees so that its toes face in the opposite direction of the kick (right).

Jump Side Kick
Assume a horse stance (left). Slide the supporting foot in so that it nearly touches the kicking foot (middle). Chamber the kicking leg in a side kick position (above right). Strike with the heel of the kicking foot. The supporting foot should pivot 90 degrees as the strike is delivered (right).

nique, you will jump as you move your supporting leg so that both feet are off the ground at the same time. Then, you will strike out with your kick, rechamber and land.

Flying Side Kick *(Dtuiyu Yup Chaki)*

This is a variation of the side kick that covers a lot of ground. Standing several yards away, run toward your target. While you are still about five feet from the target, jump into the air, chambering both legs so that your heels face the target. Kick out with your kicking leg, striking the target, and land with both feet on the ground. In Tae Kwon Do demonstrations, this technique is often done by "flying" over several seated people. Although it sounds difficult, with a little practice it is easy to do.

Roundhouse Kick *(Doll Rye Chaki)*

The roundhouse kick is used for targets that are in front of you, but the kick comes from the side instead of from the front, moving in an arc

The flying side kick.

Reverse Kick *(Dwet Chaki)*

Most kicks can be done reverse. This means that instead of kicking a target directly, you turn, pivoting around, then deliver the strike. For example, with a reverse crescent kick, instead of facing the target and sweeping your leg toward it, as you would do with a regular crescent kick, you face the target, turn away from it, pivoting on your nonkicking leg. When your back is to the target, lift your kicking leg in a sweeping arc and continue turning toward the target, striking with the edge of your foot. Although more complicated than direct kicks, reverse kicks generate great force and can be easily twice as powerful as forward or direct kicks.

In Tae Kwon Do, the term "reverse kick" usually refers to a specific kind of reverse kick — the reverse side kick. It is sometimes called a back side kick. The kick is similar to a side kick in that your leg chambers the same way and the striking surface of the foot is the same. The reverse kick can be done in any stance, but it is easiest to learn from the back stance position. Stand with the side of your body to the target. The foot closest to the target is the pivot foot. Lift the leg farthest from the target, chambering it tightly by bending the knee at least 90 degrees. The chamber for this kick is similar to the side kick. Instead of pivoting to the front and kicking, however, you spin to the back. Lean over your supporting foot to maintain your balance. Your kicking leg should be horizontal to the floor. As soon as your back is to the target, strike with your foot. The heel is the striking surface, and the toes should be parallel to the ground or turned down slightly. They should not point upward.

from outside to inside. The striking surface is the top of the foot, the instep. The roundhouse kick can be done in any stance, but to learn it, begin in a front stance. Lift your back leg from the ground and bring it in an arc from the side to the front. Your knee should be bent 90 degrees, and it should face your target. Your supporting foot should pivot so that your heel faces the target and your toes point away. As you bring your kicking leg around, the side of your leg should be horizontal to the ground. Sweeping forward, snap your foot out, striking the target with the top of your foot. Your foot should be pointed and kept tight to absorb the impact of the strike.

In Tae Kwon Do, this technique is modified when used for a board break. The toes are pulled back and the ball of the foot strikes the target. This is simply called the roundhouse kick breaking technique. It protects the foot from injury.

A short roundhouse kick moves in a straight line, not an arc, to the target. Although less powerful than a traditional roundhouse kick, it is faster. The thrust roundhouse kick is done by thrusting the hips out as the kick lands, to add power. The supporting foot pivots slightly more than usual for this powerful technique.

Kicking Secrets

As with all striking techniques, the most important secret is to kick with confidence. Although your kick may not be perfect, a confident kick can make up for many mistakes. However, it is important to practice kicking perfectly, so spend some time doing slow practice, working on correctly chambering, pivoting, striking with the appropriate part of the foot,

Front Leg Roundhouse Kick Assume a front stance (1). Lift the front leg and chamber it by bending the knee 90 degrees. Keep the inner leg parallel to the floor. The foot should be pointed. As the leg is chambered, the supporting foot should begin pivoting. At the end of the kick, the supporting foot should pivot 180 degrees (2). Snap the leg from the knee so that the foot sweeps across in an arc. Strike with the instep of the foot (3). Rechamber the kicking leg (4). Return to the starting position (5).

(1)   (2)   (3)

(4)   (5)

*Back Leg
Roundhouse Kick
Assume a front stance position (top left). Chamber the back leg (top right). Snap the kick forward, striking with the instep (below).*

(1)   (2)   (3)   (4)   (5)

Reverse Kick

Begin in a back stance. The front leg is the supporting leg (1). Turning to the back, lift and chamber the back leg by bending the back leg and ankle to 90 degrees (2). Strike directly with the heel of the foot (3). Rechamber the kick (4). Continue to turn until the kicking leg returns to the starting position (5).

rechambering and returning to the original starting position. At each workout session, practice each kick at least 10 times on each leg.

Remember the keys to any kick:

1. Chamber
2. Pivot
3. Strike (with the correct striking surface)
4. Rechamber (don't just let your foot drop when you've finished the strike)
5. Return (to your starting position).

Chambering

Several elements create a good kicking technique. The most important is a good chamber. The chamber is the cocked position of your leg that starts the kick. Each kick has a slightly different chamber position, but all chambers should be high and tight, which means the leg should rise as far as you can make it go, and the bend at the knee (if any) should be sharp and strong. Even if you are kicking to a low target area, a high and tight chamber is necessary for good power and proper technique. A high and tight chamber will also help you to kick to high target areas even if your flexibility needs work.

Rechambering

An important part of good technique is rechambering your kick after you have successfully completed your strike. This leaves you in a position to be ready to kick again quickly if you need to. For each kick, you should chamber, strike, rechamber and then return to your starting position before performing the technique again. Rechambering also allows you an extra chance to work on this essential element of kicking (the chamber).

Snapping Kicks

Each kicking technique can be improved by adding a whipping or snapping motion at the end of the kick. Instead of sweeping or

(1)   (2)   (3)   (4)   (5)

Keys to Kicking

Begin in the starting position (1). Chamber the leg by lifting it high and bending the knee sharply and to the correct angle. Pivot on the supporting foot (2). Strike with the correct striking surface (3). Rechamber the kick (4). Return to the starting position (5).

pushing with your kick, try to snap it at the moment of impact. This sharp snap generates speed and power, just the way snapping a whip works.

Speed

Speed in kicking keeps you agile and ready for your next move. If your kicks are too slow, your opponent can easily see them coming and can counter or avoid them. Even more dangerous, your opponent could grab your leg and throw you if you are too slow. For this reason, working on speed is essential. One way to improve speed and to get the necessary snap at the end of your kick is to kick as quickly as possible and then return your leg to the chamber position faster than you kicked. This requires work on pulling your kick back instead of relying on momentum. Practicing this way builds strength.

Try counting out loud for each kick. To increase speed, count faster and keep up with your count. Better yet, have someone count for you.

Practice kicks with a partner to ensure the accuracy of each kick.

The challenge is to keep up with the count by kicking quickly enough to match the pace set by the person counting.

Adding Height

The best way to add height to your kicks is to improve your flexibility. The more flexible you are, the higher you can kick. Additional leg strength also improves the height of your kicks. And, as you practice the kicks, you will learn how to create high chambers and you'll build the muscles needed to kick higher. Therefore, over time and with practice, your kicks will naturally get higher. In addition, three skills can help.

First, learn to pivot on the ball of your foot. Some martial artists end up pivoting on their heels, while others turn flat-footed. By learning to balance on the ball of the supporting foot, you'll be able to reach higher and farther with your kicks.

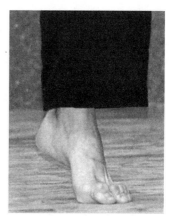

Second, lift your supporting heel off the ground as you kick. This can add several inches to your kick. For the front kick, you can go so far as to stand on your toes as you kick, since no pivot is involved. For kicks that require a pivot, you can still lift your heel off the ground and gain several inches while pivoting on the ball of your foot.

To add height to a kick, be sure to balance on the ball of the supporting foot and to lift the heel off the ground.

Finally, for kicks that require a pivot, you can add height by leaning over the supporting foot. These quick fixes can and should be used even after you've gained additional flexibility.

13

Intermediate Kicking Techniques *(Chaki)*

Once you've learned how to perform the basic kicking techniques, you can add more difficult kicks to your repertoire. Some of the intermediate kicks rely on speed rather than power, and others showcase the jumping techniques that are the hallmark of Tae Kwon Do.

Spinning Wheel Kick

Also known as the spinning heel kick, this technique looks very difficult to do but is, in fact, fairly simple. The striking surface is the back of the heel. It is performed by spinning backward, pivoting on one foot with the other leg extended straight out, knee locked. The heel of the extended leg strikes the target.

Start in a back stance with your shoulder facing the target. Like the reverse kick, you will turn to the back to strike your target. Therefore, your front leg is your supporting leg, and you will shift your weight to that leg. As

your weight is shifted to the supporting leg, extend the back leg out, keeping the knee straight. Spin on your supporting foot so that the heel of your back leg moves toward the target. Keep your heel straight by bending your ankle at a 90-degree angle. Lean over the supporting foot to maintain balance and add height to your kick. Spin through the target and return to the starting position. This technique is a high technique, so your heel should strike head or shoulder high.

Jump Front Kick *(Eidan Ap Chaki)*

This technique adds a jump to the front kick. Stand with your feet close together, facing the target. Crouch so that your knees bend about 45 degrees. The rest of your body should remain upright. Spring from the crouch, jumping into the air. As your feet leave the ground, chamber your leg and kick out with the ball of your foot. This technique works well for striking the underside of a target.

(1) (2) (3)

Spinning Wheel Kick Assume a back stance. The front leg will become the supporting leg (1). Rotate to the back (2). Lift the back leg from the floor, shifting your weight forward (3). Extend the kicking leg straight out and sweep in a circle (4). Strike with the back of the heel (5). Continue rotating and return to the starting position (6).

(4) (5) (6)

Jump Front Kick Spring into the air, chambering the kicking leg tightly prior to striking with the ball of the foot.

Jump Reverse Kick *(Eidan Dwet Chaki)*

This technique adds a jump to the reverse kick. Stand in a horse stance with your shoulder facing the target. Bend your knees slightly. As you jump, chamber your back leg and kick the target with your heel. Return to the starting position.

Jump Roundhouse Kick
(Eidan Doll Rye Chaki)

This technique adds a jump to the roundhouse kick. Stand with your feet together, facing your target. Crouch so that your knees bend about 45 degrees. The rest of your body should be upright and straight. As you spring from the crouch, push off with your supporting foot, pivoting slightly to position your kick correctly. Chamber your kicking leg and sweep with your kick, striking with the top of your foot.

Hooking Kick *(Ap Hurya Chaki)*

The hooking kick can be done from any stance, but it is easiest to learn from the horse stance. The striking surface is the back of the heel. The kicking foot travels parallel to the floor and snaps back to the target, making a hooking motion. Stand in a horse stance with your shoulder facing the target. The leg closest to the target is the kicking leg. Lift your kicking leg and chamber as you would for a side kick. Instead of kicking with the bottom of your foot, however, you will be striking with the back of your heel. Therefore, as you extend your leg and straighten your knee, your foot will go past the target. Then, snap your foot to the back, through the target, with a hooking motion. The back of your heel strikes the target.

Jump Roundhouse Kick
Spring into the air (left). Chamber the kicking leg (middle). Strike with the instep of the foot (right).

Jump Reverse Kick
Assume a strong back stance (right). Spring into the air and turn to the back (below left). Strike directly with the heel of the foot (below right).

(1)   (2)   (3)

Hooking Kick
Assume a horse stance (1). Chamber the leg by lifting it and bending the knee at a 90-degree angle (2). Snap the leg out, extending the knee (3). Hook your heel back, bending sharply at the knee (4). Return to the starting position (5).

(4)

(5)

Hooking Kick, Front Stance
Assume a front stance (left). Lift the back leg, chamber and extend (middle). Hook the heel back toward the target, striking with the back of the heel (right).

Jump Hooking Kick
(Eidan Hurya Chaki)

This technique adds a jump to the hooking kick. The jump is performed in a similar way to the jump side kick. Stand in a horse stance with your shoulder facing the target. With your supporting leg, step toward your kicking leg. Lift your kicking leg and perform the hooking kick. As you become more proficient, turn the step into a jump, so that you are jumping toward your target, keeping both feet off the ground, then executing the hooking kick.

Reverse Jump Hooking Kick

The hooking kick can be made into a reverse hooking kick by rotating to the back and then striking. It can also be made into a reverse jump hooking kick by adding a rotation to the jump hooking kick.

Jump Spinning Wheel Kick

This is the most difficult of the intermediate kicks, but with practice it can be mastered. Stand in a back stance with your shoulder facing the target. Bend your knees slightly and twist forward at the waist. Jump from this position, untwisting and springing into the target with your spinning wheel kick. Both feet should leave the ground as you move toward your target.

Jumping Kick Secrets

The best way to work on a jump kick is to break it into its various parts. A jump front kick can be broken into the jump and the front kick. Practice jumping first without worrying about the front kick. This means standing with your feet together, facing the target. Crouch, bending your knees about 45 degrees, then

Jump Hooking Kick
Assume a horse stance *(1)*.
Slide the supporting foot
toward the kicking leg.
Chamber the kicking leg
(2). Extend the kicking leg
(3). Hook the foot back so
the back of the heel
strikes the target *(4)*.

(1)

(2)

(3)

(4)

(1)   (2)   (3)

Reverse Jump Hooking Kick

Begin in a back stance (1). Turn to the back (2). Lift the kicking leg (3). Spring into the air and hook back with the foot, striking with the heel (4). Follow through with the kick (5). Return to the starting position (6).

(4)   (5)   (6)

*Jump Spinning
Wheel Kick
Rotate to the back and jump
into the spinning wheel kick.*

(1)   (2)

springing as high as you can. Continue practicing this until you can easily jump high and maintain your balance. Then put the jump and the kick together, going slowly at first, then faster as you become better at it. Each jump kick has a slightly different jump, but as you master each jump, the others become easier.

For the side kick and the reverse kick, try jumping and tucking your legs as tightly under you as possible. Try to make your calves touch your thighs. This helps you jump higher and it puts your kicking leg in a better position to chamber and kick from. Plyometric drills will also improve your ability to jump (see PartVI, Chapter 23.)

Practice Jumping

14

Elbow and Knee Striking Techniques (Pahl-Koom-Chi Chigi and *Moohrup Chaki)*

In addition to striking with the hands and the feet, Tae Kwon Do practitioners learn to strike with their elbows and knees. This increases the ability to succeed in a confrontation.

Elbow Strikes (Pahl-Koom-Chi Chigi)

There are two striking areas on the elbow: the front of the elbow and the point of the elbow. Every elbow strike uses one or the other of these striking surfaces.

Forward Elbow Strike

The simplest elbow strike uses the front of the elbow to strike. Although this elbow strike can be performed in any stance, it is easiest to learn in a front stance. The target is directly in front of you. Bend the forward arm tightly. Keep your arm horizontal to the floor. Pivoting at the waist, turn back so that you are reaching behind you with the elbow. Then uncoil at the waist, sweeping your elbow forward and through the target.

Reverse Elbow Strike

The reverse elbow strike uses the point of the elbow as the striking surface. The target is directly behind you. Bend the arm so that it is at a 90-degree angle, with your forearm horizontal to the floor. Make your hand a fist. Reach forward slightly with your arm, then shove backward using the palm of your opposing hand to help push. The point of your elbow should drive backward, striking the target.

(1)

(2)

(3)

(4)

(5)

Forward Elbow Strike
Assume a front stance. Chamber your arm by cocking the elbow tightly and holding the arm horizontal to the floor (1). Sweep the arm forward (2). Continue sweeping while twisting into the strike at the waist (3). Strike with the front of the elbow (4). The elbow strike in action (5).

(1) (2) (3) (4)

Reverse Elbow Strike
Bend the striking arm at a 90-degree angle, keeping your forearm parallel to the floor (1). Make your hand into a fist. Reach slightly forward with the striking arm (2). Shove your arm backward, using the palm of the opposing hand to help push (3). Slide backward to add power to the strike (4).

You can increase the power of this technique by sliding backward as you execute the elbow strike, which puts the entire weight of your body behind it.

Upward Elbow Strike

This technique uses the front of the elbow as the striking surface. Bend the arm tightly so that the point of the elbow faces the floor.

Upward Elbow Strike
Begin in the front stance. Bend the elbow tightly at your side (1). Sweep the elbow upward (2). Strike with the front of the elbow (3).

(1) (2) (3)

113

(1) (2) (3) (4)

Downward Elbow Strike
Assume a front stance. Bend the arm to make a 90-degree angle (1). Lift the arm up (2). Drive downward with the arm (3). Strike with the point of the elbow (4).

Make your hand into a fist. Reach back slightly with your elbow, then drive the elbow upward, so that your fist moves to the side of your head near your ear. Strike with the front (now the top) part of the elbow.

You can increase the power of this technique by sliding or stepping forward as you execute it. This puts the entire weight of your body behind the technique.

Downward Elbow Strike

This technique uses the point of the elbow as the striking surface. Bend your arm so that it makes a 90-degree angle. The upper arm should be horizontal to the floor. Make your hand a fist. Reach up slightly with your arm, then drive directly downward through the target, striking with the point of the elbow.

Side Elbow Strike

This technique uses the point of the elbow as the striking surface. The target is to the side. Bend your arm so that it creates a 90-degree angle. Make your hand a fist. Bring the

arm slightly across your body. Drive your elbow to the side, thrusting the point of your elbow into the target. You can use the palm of the opposite hand to help push the arm through.

To increase the power of this technique, step or slide to the side as you perform it. This puts the weight of your body into the technique.

Knee Strikes (Moohrup Chaki)

Knee strikes are fairly straightforward; simply strike the target with your knee. When doing knee strikes, increase the power of the technique by pulling the target toward your knee while driving your knee into it.

Straight Knee Strike

This technique uses the front of the kneecap as the striking surface. In a front stance, swing the back leg forward and bend your knee to a 90-degree angle. Drive the knee directly

*Side Elbow Strike
Assume a horse stance. Cock the elbow 90 degrees, keeping the arm horizontal to the floor (left). Drive the elbow to the side, thrusting the point of the elbow into the target (right).*

into the target. This strike works for middle section (the groin area) and high section (the face). To knee strike to the face, it helps to grab the opponent's head and pull it down toward your knee as you strike forward.

Roundhouse Knee Strike

Like the roundhouse kick, this technique approaches from the side. In a front stance, lift the back leg from the floor. Bend the knee at a 90-degree angle, keeping the inner side of the leg turned toward the floor. Sweep from the side across your body. Drive the knee into your target, holding your target and pulling it toward your knee if possible.

Elbow and Knee Strike Secrets

Although elbow and knee strikes aren't allowed in freestyle sparring because they are so dangerous, they are very effective techniques

*Straight Knee Strike
Assume a front stance (left). Bend the knee to a 90-degree angle (middle). Drive the knee directly into the target (right).*

Roundhouse Knee Strike
Assume a front stance (left). Sweep the knee in from the side, driving the knee into the target (right).

for confrontations. To improve knee and elbow strikes, think speed. Martial artists often push with their elbows and knees, using power to make the technique work. But these techniques rely on speed. Strike as quickly as possible and return to the starting position, prepared to strike again. Return to the starting position faster than you struck for maximum effect.

15

Sweeps, Takedowns and Throws

Sweeps, takedowns and throws are exciting but dangerous techniques in Tae Kwon Do. If you plan to practice these techniques with a partner, always choose a safe place with a padded mat. Be sure your partner understands exactly what you plan to do so that he or she doesn't get hurt. This doesn't mean your partner shouldn't offer resistance because you do need a realistic idea of how the technique works, but it does mean your partner should know which direction he or she is going to fall and where you are going to attack. Never drop someone that you are throwing. Always hold on to him, help him down and then help him back up again. (This is the Tenet of courtesy.) Of course, in an actual confrontation, you wouldn't hold on to an opponent during a throw; the harder your attacker hits the floor, the better.

Falling Correctly

Practicing takedown techniques can lead to injury if you don't know how to fall. Often, our instinct is to put a hand out to break a fall. When practicing takedown techniques, however, this could result in a broken arm or at least a sprained wrist.

When being thrown to the front, you don't want to land on your face or directly on your hand. Keep your head lifted and your face turned to the side. Thrusting the arm and shoulder forward can help absorb the impact where it will do the least damage. Instead of landing directly on your hand, reach forward with it, bending at the elbow. Move your hand and arm to slide yourself forward as you fall.

Falls to the back should be absorbed with the hip and shoulder. Never let your head touch the ground; tuck your chin tightly to your chest. Don't extend your arm straight out to the back to catch yourself. Land first on your hip and shoulder, then slap your hand, palm down, on the ground, extending your arm.

Takedowns to Counter Hand Strikes

Most takedown techniques are counters to punches. That is, they are done as a response to someone throwing a punch (or other hand striking technique) at you. This is because most confrontations start with hand techniques, such as a punch, and you can effectively end a confrontation after one blow if you use a throwing technique.

Practice takedowns using a mat.

Falling Forward
Reach forward with your arm, bending it at the elbow. Slide forward to minimize impact.

Falling Backward
Absorb the impact on your hip and shoulder. Be sure to tuck your chin in. Slap your palm to the ground to prevent landing on your hand or elbow.

(1)

(2)

(3)

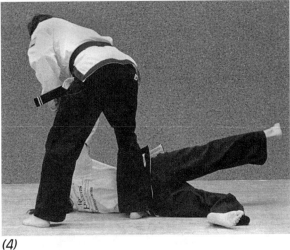
(4)

Shoulder Takedown
Assume your partner is punching toward your nose (1). Step away from the punch, toward your partner's body. Grab the wrist and shoulder of the punching arm (2). Slide your foot behind your partner's. Push on your partner's shoulder and hook his or her foot out with your leg (3). Throw your partner to the ground (4).

Shoulder Takedown

Assume the opponent is punching toward your nose. Step away from the punch, toward the opponent's body. Block the punch and grab the wrist of the punching hand with your nearest hand. Grab the shoulder of the punching arm with your other hand. Slide your closest foot forward, placing it behind the opponent's leg. Pushing on the shoulder, hook the opponent's leg out from under with your leg, throwing him or her to the ground.

Elbow Takedown

Assume the opponent is punching toward your nose. Step away from the punch, toward the opponent's body. Block and grab the wrist of the punching hand with your nearest hand. With your other hand, grab the opponent's elbow, digging your fingers into the joint. Bend the opponent's elbow. Then, slide your nearest foot behind the opponent's foot. Pull up on the opponent's elbow. This will put your opponent off balance, allowing you to hook his or her leg out from under, throwing him or her to the ground.

Hip Throw

Assume the opponent is punching to your nose. Block with your outside arm as you spin away from the punch; your back should face the opponent's body and your feet should straddle your opponent's nearest foot. Next,

119

Elbow Takedown

Assume your partner is punching toward your nose. Grab her wrist and elbow (1). Dig your fingers into the elbow joint and bend the elbow (2). Pull your partner's elbow upward to off-balance him or her (3). Slide your foot behind your partner's leg (4). Throw your partner over your leg (5).

(1)

(4)

Hip Throw

Assume your partner is punching toward your nose. Step away from the punch, moving toward your partner's body (1). Block your partner's punching arm with your opposite arm (2). Straddle your partner's foot. Your back should be facing your partner (3). Drive your elbow into your partner's solar plexus (4). Drive your other elbow into your partner's ribs (5). Reach back and grab your partner's shoulder and upper arm (6). Pull your partner across your hip (7). Throw your partner to the ground (8).

(2)

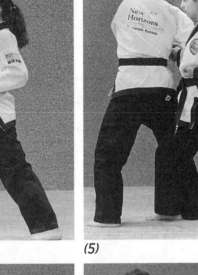

(5)

(7)

(3)

(6)

(8)

(1)

(2)

(3)

(4)

Ankle Sweep

Assume your opponent is punching toward your nose. Step away from the punch (1). Grab your partner's wrist (2). Reaching down, sweep in a circular motion, grabbing your partner's ankle (3). Knock or pull the ankle out from under your partner, throwing him or her to the ground (4).

(1)

(2)

(3)

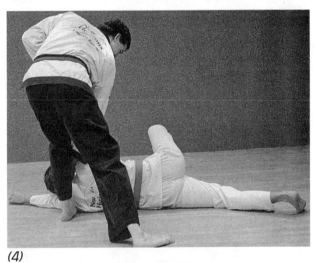

(4)

Head Throw

Assume your opponent is punching toward your nose. Step away from the punch (1). Grab your partner's wrist and lift the arm straight up. With your free hand, grab your partner's neck (2). Push your partner's head down toward the arm (3). Continue pushing until your partner loses balance and falls to the ground (4).

drive your elbow into the opponent's solar plexus. Twist at the waist and reach behind you. Grab the opponent's upper arm and shoulder. Uncoil and pull the opponent forward against your hip, which works as a pivot point. Throw the opponent forward.

Ankle Sweep

Assume the opponent is punching to your nose. Step away from the punch, moving toward the opponent's body. Grab the wrist of the punching hand with your nearest hand. Reaching down, sweep in a circular motion,

(1)

(2)

(3)

(4)

Takedown to Counter a Roundhouse Kick

As your partner performs a roundhouse kick, block the kick by guarding the middle and high sections (1). Grab your partner's kicking leg and upper arm (2). Step forward, sliding your foot behind your partner's supporting leg (3). Throw your partner to the ground (4).

knocking or pulling the opponent's nearest ankle away. Throw your opponent to the ground.

Head Throw

Assume the opponent is punching to your nose. Step away from the punch, moving toward the opponent's body. Grab the wrist of the punching hand with your nearest hand. Lift the arm straight up. Place the palm of your free hand on the side of your opponent's neck nearest his or her punching arm. Push the opponent's head in a circular motion toward the opponent's arm, which you are still holding up in the air. Continue pushing until the opponent's body is partly turned away from you and the opponent loses his or her balance. Allow the opponent to fall to the ground.

Takedowns to Counter Kicks

Using a takedown as a counter to a kick can be dangerous except under certain circumstances. When a takedown is used to counter a punch, the opponent's punch can be avoided or deflected and the takedown performed with little danger. However, if a kick is coming straight at you, and you avoid or deflect it, you won't be in any position to perform a takedown technique. You will be at kicking distance, which is too far away to perform a takedown without running the risk of getting struck. If you don't block or counter the kick, instead trying to perform a takedown, you will probably be struck. Therefore, takedowns don't work well to counter kicks, although advanced Tae Kwon Do practitioners can find ways to do so. The exception to this general rule is for kicks that come at an angle from the side instead of from straight ahead. This includes the roundhouse kick and the spinning wheel kick, both of which can be countered with a throw.

Takedown to Counter a Roundhouse or Spinning Wheel Kick

This technique is simple to perform. As your opponent performs the roundhouse kick or spinning wheel kick, block the technique with your hands. Then, grab the opponent's kicking leg. As the opponent balances on one leg, step forward quickly, grab the opponent's shirt, and hook the supporting leg out from under him or her.

Sweep, Takedown and Throw Secrets

As with other Tae Kwon Do techniques, the secret to sweeps, takedowns and throws is speed. The more quickly you execute the technique, the more likely you will do it effectively. By being quick, you will also avoid the possibility of the opponent resisting the throw. Although you will practice the techniques slowly and carefully at first, as you build confidence, you can move more quickly (but carefully). With practice, you will be able to guide your opponent's momentum and use the energy it generates against him. This makes throws, takedowns and sweeps easier to accomplish with less effort and power.

16

Board Breaking

Board and block breaking is an important element of Tae Kwon Do. Done with the same techniques the student has already learned and used, such as kicks and punches, board breaking serves three purposes.

- Board breaking demonstrates power. In practice, you can't kick your partner full power; even if you use targets, it can be difficult to feel how powerful your techniques are. Breaking a one-inch board, which is equal to a person's rib, can make the practitioner feel more confident.

- It demonstrates proper technique. Boards don't break unless the breaking technique is done correctly. If you are trying to break a board with your side kick and you hit the board with your toes instead of your heel, you won't have any luck. Thus, you learn if you are doing your techniques effectively.

- Board breaking improves mental discipline. It can be a challenge mentally to break a board. You might be afraid that it will hurt or that you won't be able to do it. Board breaking is often harder to do mentally than it is to do physically. Overcoming these mental blocks and doubts is an important part of board breaking.

Board Breaking Secrets

Although board and block breaking should only be done under the supervision of a qualified black belt instructor, there are a few pointers that can help.

Board Placement

First, make sure the board is being held correctly. The correct hold is different for each technique. For the side kick, spinning wheel kick, reverse kick and hooking kick, the board is held with the target surface perpendicular to the floor, the grain running horizontally. For the axe kick and front kick, the board is held parallel to the ground. For the roundhouse kick, the board is held at a 45-degree angle.

Always set the board at the right height for you, allowing for any surge of adrenalin that might be forthcoming. Aim for and strike the center of the board. For most kicks, this means the back of your shoulder should be lined up with the front edge of the board.

Board Holders

Board holders should be in a strong front stance, with space for your leg or arm to follow

127

(1)

(2)

(3)

(4)

(5)

(6)

(7)

The photos on this page demonstrate a board break with a jump side kick technique.

These photos illustrate the proper way to hold a board for a side kick.

through. For beginning and intermediate breaks, two holders should be used. They should stand shoulder to shoulder, back legs overlapping. Each holder's inner arm should grasp the top of the board. The outer arm should grasp the bottom of the board. The board should be held as securely as possible. If the holder is afraid of getting hit or flinches as you perform your technique, this person should not hold boards. Board holders should look away from the board as soon as you signal your intention to break, which is done by giving a kihop or yell.

The Kihop

Always kihop or yell before the start of your board breaking attempt. This helps you summon your chi, or inner energy, so that you can focus all of your attention and effort on breaking the board. It also serves to warn your board holders that you are about to begin the break. This way they can prepare themselves for the

impact. As a courtesy, be sure to bow to your board holders before and after the break.

Speed Versus Power

A common mistake Tae Kwon Do practitioners make is assuming that the more powerful the technique, the more likely they are to break the board. Thus, they may assume that bigger people have less trouble than smaller people. They also push at the board instead of snapping it. This assumption can lead to frustration and discouragement. Why? Because the main element in board breaking is *not* power or strength, but speed. The faster your hand or fist hits the board, the more likely you are to break it. However, some people work on speed to the exclusion of power; some weight must also be put behind your techniques to break a board. The key is to strike quickly and confidently — although that's easier said than done.

Correct Targeting

Another common mistake Tae Kwon Do practitioners make when attempting to board break is thinking of the board itself as the target. This means they don't follow through, so their technique stops at the board without breaking it. By visualizing a target behind the board, and aiming there, the Tae Kwon Do practitioner can more successfully break boards. Therefore, imagine that your target is about four or six inches behind the board and that you must strike quickly and confidently to that target.

Mental Preparation

Finally, another common problem is a lack of mental preparedness. Martial artists who allow fear and doubt to enter their minds before a board break will have great difficulty performing the board break. But it is not uncommon, especially for beginning martial artists, to be afraid of committing themselves to the board break, so they stop at the board or just short of it, bouncing off it without breaking it. This leads to bruises, frustration and fear of trying. When breaking, mentally prepare and be ready to put your entire self into the break, going as fast as you can, as hard as you can.

The proper way to hold a board for an axe kick and front kick.

The photos at left depict the proper way to hold a board for a roundhouse kick.

Part III

17

Step Sparring
(Bo Dae Ryun)

Uses of Step Sparring

Step sparring is a method of practicing fighting techniques in combination to prepare for freestyle sparring or for possible confrontations. Step sparring takes place under more controlled circumstances than freestyle sparring, so it is a good way to practice different techniques you haven't used before and for trying different combinations of techniques to see if they work the way you want them to.

Step sparring also helps improve timing and countering skills, both of which are essential to freestyle sparring. In step sparring, you can also use techniques that aren't allowed in freestyle sparring, so you can create more realistic fight scenarios.

Defensive Nature of Martial Arts

Step sparring is usually taught as a defensive technique. The Tae Kwon Do practitioner is confronted by an attacker who punches. The martial artist blocks the punch and steps back, saying something to the effect of "I don't want to fight." Only when it is clear that the attacker won't stop does the martial artist counter the punch with a series of techniques meant to stop the attacker.

How to Begin

Step sparring is easiest if you work with a partner, but if you don't have one, you can practice shadow sparring. Or use a heavy bag as your partner. If you do use a partner, remember to work with care. As you practice the techniques, use good control. Although it is acceptable to touch your partner with your strikes, blocks and kicks, you should never exert full force. Limit contact to light touch. When you become more confident in your skills, you and your partner may agree to heavier contact, but special care should always be taken to avoid injury.

The Attack

Start by having your partner punch to your nose. As you grow more proficient, vary the routine by using different hand techniques, such as knife hand strikes, punches to the middle section and the like. Once you are comfortable with this, have your partner strike with kicks, again using a variety of kicks to a variety of target areas.

Of course, you can practice these counters even without a partner; you simply have to imagine that an opponent is punching or kicking, and you are responding. You can use a heavy bag as a target or you can shadow spar.

The Block

The first technique that you should use when your partner punches is a block. This emphasizes the defensive nature of martial arts. As you learn the different blocks, use them to counter the different strikes your partner uses. In the beginning, it is easiest to use a knife hand block to counter the high punch.

The Counter

Once you've blocked your partner's strike, you'll counter with two or three techniques that flow smoothly. Since you'll be starting from farther away and moving in, it makes sense to start with kicking techniques and then move to hand techniques. Your partner should stand his or her ground (don't hit your partner — use self-control.) Having both partners moving back and forth is done in freestyle sparring, not step sparring, since it's more dangerous and requires more care.

When you have finished your techniques, kihop so that your partner knows you've finished. It is always courteous to let your partner know ahead of time when you are going to do an unexpected technique like a knee strike or a throw. Be sure to take turns attacking and defending (the person who throws the punch is the attacker; the person who blocks and counters is the defender).

Step Sparring Drills

The following step sparring drills are included to get you started. Go through these several times until you feel comfortable with each sequence, then add your own variations. Once you think you're ready to strike out on your own, feel free to make up your own step sparring sequences.

Some Tae Kwon Do practitioners develop a set of step sparring sequences that they master and which cover different kinds of punches and kicks. They practice their set of step sparring techniques at each workout. This helps them feel they would react more quickly in the case of an actual attack. Other Tae Kwon Do practitioners try to respond to step sparring with fresh techniques each time, trying to react to their partner's kicks or punches without thinking about it. They feel this would be more helpful in an actual attack, where you might not be able to recall your memorized response to a left hook to the ribs. You might consider doing both: develop a set of step sparring sequences that you like and practice them until they become effortless but also set aside time now and then to practice simply reacting to your partner's techniques.

On all step sparring sequences, the person who is attacking first should always kihop before performing the technique. This alerts the defender to be prepared. By the same token, the defender should also kihop after the attacker does, to show that he or she *is* prepared. This helps to prevent accidental contact and helps prevent injuries. To make the step sparring scenario more realistic, you might try having both partners signal that they are ready. Once the signal is given, the attacker can wait for whatever length of time he or she wishes before attacking. This makes it harder for the defender to anticipate the attack and makes it more realistic while at the same time helping to keep step sparring safe.

For the following drills, the attacking partner should begin in a front stance with the left leg forward. He or she should perform a low block over the left leg, then kihop to show readiness. The defending partner should stand naturally in a ready stance. After hearing the attacker's kihop, the defending partner should kihop to signal readiness. Then, the attacking partner should step forward into a front stance with the right leg forward, at the same time performing a straight punch with the right hand. The straight punch should be aimed at the defender's nose.

Once the following drills have been learned and are understood, change the attacking sequence using different punches, stances and striking technique. Remember, however, to have both partners kihop to show that they are ready.

To practice step sparring, the attacker should begin in a front stance with the left leg forward. The attacker should perform a low block over the front leg. The defender should stand in a chunbee or ready stance. Both partners should kihop to show their readiness.

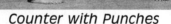

Counter with Punches

As the attacking partner steps forward and punches with the right hand, step to your left and block the arm out of the way by performing a palm strike with the left hand (left). Deliver a punch to the ribs with the right hand (middle). Finish by punching with the left hand (right).

Counter with Punches

As your partner punches to your head, step to the left, away from the punch. Block the punch away with the palm of your left hand, using a palm strike. Punch to the ribs with your right hand, then with your left. Kihop to signal the end of the sequence.

As a variation, perform a knife hand block with your left hand when the partner punches. Then step to the right, away from the punch. Punch to the solar plexus with your right hand. Keeping your partner's punching hand blocked, punch to the face with your right hand. Kihop to signal the end of the sequence.

(1) (2)

(3) (4)

Counter with Punches Variation
As your partner punches, perform a knife hand block (1). Step to the right, chambering both fists (2). Punch to the solar plexus with the right hand, while blocking the opponent's punching arm again (3). Punch again with the right hand, this time to the face (4).

Counter with Double Punch and Kick

As your partner punches toward your head, step to the left, away from your partner's body. Punch to the ribs with your right hand. Then punch to the ribs with your left hand. Finally, perform a roundhouse kick with your right leg, aiming for your partner's midsection. Kihop to signal the end of the sequence.

As a variation, use a side kick to the ribs instead of the roundhouse kick.

Counter with Elbow Strike

As your partner punches toward your nose, perform an outside-inside block with your right arm. As you block, step over your partner's forward foot, so that you are straddling it. Your

(1) (2) (3) (4)

Counter with Double Punch and Kick
As your partner punches, step to the left and punch to the ribs with the right hand (1). Punch to the ribs with the left hand (2). Finish with a roundhouse kick to the solar plexus (3). As a variation, use a sidekick instead of a roundhouse kick (4).

back should be to your partner, one foot on each side of his or her forward foot. Drive your left elbow into your partner's solar plexus. Kihop to signal the end of the sequence.

As a variation, do a double elbow strike. Drive your left elbow into your partner's solar plexus, then twist at the waist and drive your right elbow into your partner's ribs or kidney area (whichever you can reach). As a further variation, add a shoulder throw.

Counter with Knife Hand Strike and Knee Strike

As your partner punches toward your nose, step right, avoiding the punch. Block the punch by using your left hand to perform a knife hand

(1) (2)

(3) (4)

Counter with Elbow Strike

As your partner punches to your head, step to the right (1). Block the punching arm with an outside-inside block while stepping over your partner's forward foot (2). With your back to your partner and your feet straddling your partner's forward foot, chamber your arm for a backward elbow strike (3). Deliver a backward elbow strike (4).

(1)

(2)

(3)

(4)

As a variation to the elbow strike, perform a double elbow strike.

(1)

(2)

(3)

(4)

As a further variation to the elbow strike, add a shoulder throw.

(1)

(2)

Counter with Knife Hand Strike and Knee Strike

As your partner punches, step to the right. Chamber your hands as you would for a double knife hand block (1). Block the punch with your left hand using a knife hand block. With your right hand, strike to your partner's neck (2). Grab your partner's neck and pull forward. Deliver a knee to the solar plexus (3).

(3)

block. Step forward with your left leg and strike to the neck with a 45-degree knife hand strike using your right hand. Grab the back of your partner's neck and pull him or her toward your knee. Drive your right knee into the partner's solar plexus. Kihop to signal the end of the sequence.

Counter with Palm Strike and Knee Strike

As your partner punches toward your head, perform a high block with your left hand. Then, perform a palm strike to your partner's nose, using your right hand. Next, reaching with both hands, grab the back of your partner's neck and

141

(1)

(2)

(3)

(4)

Counter with Palm Strike and Knee Strike
As your partner punches to your head, peform a high block (1). Perform a palm strike to your partner's head (2). Grab your partner's neck and shoulders (3). Pull your partner down as you deliver a knee strike (4).

pull his or her head toward your knee. Drive your right knee into the partner's face. Kihop to signal the end of the sequence.

Counter with Side Kick, Reverse Kick

As your partner punches toward your head, step to the left away from your partner's body.

Block the punch by performing a knife hand block with your right hand, pushing your partner's arm toward his or her own body. Perform a side kick with your right leg, striking to your partner's ribs. Set your kicking foot down, turn and execute a reverse kick with your left foot, striking to your partner's ribs. Kihop to signal the end of the sequence.

(2)

(1)

Counter with Side Kick and Reverse Kick
As your partner punches, step to your left.
Perform a knife hand block to the punching
arm (1). Deliver a side kick with your right leg
(2). Set the kicking foot down (3). Turn and
perform a reverse kick (4).

(3)

(4)

(1)

(2)

Counter with Hooking Kick and Roundhouse Kick
As your partner punches, perform a block by doing an inside-outside crescent kick to the punching arm with your left leg (1). As your blocking foot lands, perform a hooking kick with your right leg (2). Then perform a roundhouse kick with the same leg (3).

(3)

Counter with Hooking Kick and Roundhouse Kick

As your partner punches toward your head, step slightly back with your left leg. Bring your left leg up in an inside-outside crescent kick, knocking your partner's punching hand away.

As you land on your left foot, bring your right foot up and perform a hooking kick to the side of your partner's face. Before setting the foot down, rechamber and perform a roundhouse kick to the opposite side of your partner's face. Kihop to signal the end of the sequence.

Create Your Own Step Sparring Sequences

As you become more proficient with step sparring, create your own step sparring sequences, working out how to avoid a strike and then how to counter it. Because step sparring is used to practice for real confrontations, consider combining multiple techniques together, in case the first one or two techniques aren't effective. In a real fight, you should never rely on one great knockout strike, but you should always be prepared to continue fighting with other techniques.

(1)

Create Step Sparring Drills
As an example, when your partner punches, block and grab the punching arm and deliver a punch to the solar plexus (1). Then think of a kick to add. For example, a front kick to the groin (2,3). Then think of another kick to add (see next page).

(2)

(3)

For example, a roundhouse kick. As you become more skilled, you should be able to perform the front kick and the roundhouse kick without setting the kicking leg down between kicks.

18

Freestyle Sparring
(Ja Yu Dae Ryun)

Freestyle sparring is a method of fighting a partner under a specific set of rules. Each person attacks and defends continuously, according to his or her abilities, using Tae Kwon Do techniques. Unlike step sparring, both partners move about, trying to score points by landing an unblocked strike. Freestyle sparring matches run the gamut from slow-paced, where partners spar lightly, feeling each other out, to high intensity, where partners move and counter almost faster than you can watch.

Legal Target Areas

Although freestyle sparring is as close to a real fight as martial arts gets, there are still rules about what kinds of techniques you can use and which areas of the body you can strike. In Tae Kwon Do, the legal target areas are the sides of the head (not the nose or throat), and the chest, including the ribs and side. Anything below the belt is illegal, as is anything to the back, the knees or the ankles. No takedowns, sweeps or throws are allowed.

Any kick is allowed to the head or the body. All hand techniques are allowed to the body, but only advanced practitioners can use hand techniques to the head. Punches to the head are never allowed, as they are too dangerous. Elbow strikes and knee strikes are not allowed for the same reason.

Point Scoring

In Tae Kwon Do competitions, freestyle sparring matches are popular. Matches are won by landing the most unblocked strikes. Depending on the competition, points may be awarded in different ways, but usually one point is awarded for any hand or foot technique to the body and two points are awarded for any foot technique to the head. In some Tae Kwon Do tournaments, the difficulty of the punch or kick that landed unblocked is also awarded points, so the more difficult the technique, the more points are scored.

Two-Minute Matches

Most practice matches run continuously for two minutes. This is because tournament sparring is scored in two-minute rounds and such practice prepares fighters for competition. Although two minutes does not seem like a lot of time at first, it is once you try. Usually practice is conducted by having several two-minute

Sparring (right and below) improves your Tae Kwon Do skills.

Extra stretching before sparring can help you do those high kicks.

matches with 30 or 60 seconds of rest between. This builds endurance. Longer or shorter matches can add variety to sparring practice, so there is no set length of time a practice match has to last.

Practicing with a Partner

If you plan to practice sparring with a partner, you should be supervised by a qualified black belt. This helps ensure safety and appropriate practice. Beginners should always start slowly with no contact. As confidence is gained and you learn how to control your techniques, you can go faster, adding more and more techniques to your sparring arsenal. In Tae Kwon Do, some contact is expected during sparring, but you should never make contact with your partner unless you both agree to the amount and intensity of the contact.

Safety Equipment

During sparring, Tae Kwon Do practitioners should wear at least a minimal amount of safety equipment to help prevent injuries. Usually, foot pads and hand pads plus headgear and mouth guards are required. Men should wear groin protectors. Chest protectors, shin guards and forearm guards can also be used.

Fighting Range

The most important concept to learn when sparring is the concept of fighting range. What this means is that, depending on how close you are to your sparring partner, you will use different techniques. If you are several feet from your partner, you are in kicking range, and kicking techniques will be most effective. If you are within a foot or two of your partner, you are in punching range and hand striking techniques

Punching Range

Kicking Range

will be most effective. If you are too far from your partner for a kick to be effective, you are out of range and need to close the gap. Many beginners spar several feet away from their partners so that they don't make accidental contact, but you should close this gap as you become more confident. Alternatively, fighters sometimes get too close to each other, and then no techniques are effective. When this happens, you have to move back into fighting range. Moving into and out of the different fighting ranges requires footwork. Footwork is one area of sparring that can easily be practiced without a partner.

Footwork (Bal Ohmkigi)

Footwork is simply the placement of your feet as you spar. Frequently, as you spar, you won't even be aware of where your feet are, because you are more concerned with whether you'll be able to kick or punch in time to take advantage of an opening. However, your footwork is an important element of sparring. If you are proficient with your footwork, you can move into and out of range effortlessly, and you'll be able to evade and counter your partner's techniques much more easily.

To practice footwork, repeat each footwork pattern several times. Then, ask your partner to slowly punch or kick while you perform a footwork pattern to evade or counter the technique. Speed up the practice as you become more comfortable moving your feet.

Forward Stepping

Also called straight stepping. This is simply moving in a straight line toward your target. Forward stepping is used when you are too far away to kick, or if you are in kicking range and you want to move to punching range. The best way to forward step is to slide your front foot forward, then pull your back foot forward. Practice small, quick slides toward your target. To vary forward stepping, try kicking with your front foot, using a front kick, then sliding your back foot forward as you land.

Backward Stepping

Backward stepping is simply moving in a straight line away from your target. This technique is used when you are in too close to use any techniques, when you are in punching range and want to move to kicking range, and when you want to move completely out of range. The best way to backward step is to slide your back foot backward, then pull your front foot backward. Practice small, quick slides away from your target. Forward stepping and backward stepping can be combined to move you into and out of fighting range. They should be practiced together by making small, quick slides toward your target and then making small,

Forward Stepping
Begin in a fighting stance. Slide the front foot forward (left). Slide the back foot forward (middle). Step forward with the front foot. You should be in another fighting stance (right).

quick slides away from your target. The faster you can move your feet, the more versatile and agile a fighter you'll be.

Side Stepping

This technique is used to travel at a 90-degree angle to your partner. It is used when your partner is moving or kicking straight at you. A quick side step gets you out of the way of the technique and allows you to counter with your own technique. A side step is done the same way as a forward step, except of course you slide to the left or right instead of forward. Often, as your partner moves forward with a technique, you can side step it and then kick or punch to your partner's now-exposed ribs.

Angle Stepping

This technique is used to travel at a 45-degree angle to your partner. It is used when your partner is kicking at you from the side, with a roundhouse kick or a spinning wheel kick. A quick angle step gets you out of the way and allows you to set up a countering technique. You must move in the direction away from the kick for this step to be effective.

Pivot Stepping

The pivot step is used to avoid a technique coming straight at you while you move in toward your partner or away from your partner. To pivot step toward your partner, push off with your rear foot, and pivot in a circle on your front foot. Your partner's technique will slide right by you and you will be in a position to strike immediately. To pivot step away from your partner, push off with your front foot, and pivot in a circle on your back foot. Your partner's technique will slide right by you and you will be out of range of any further techniques. This can be used when your partner is overwhelming you and you need a moment to regroup.

Crossover Stepping

To cover a lot of ground while keeping your guard up, use the crossover step. Bring your back foot over your front foot, so that

Side Stepping
Assume a fighting stance (left). Take a quick step to the side to avoid a strike (right).

Angle Stepping
Assume a fighting stance (left). Step away at a 45-degree angle, avoiding the opponent's strike (right).

they cross. Then slide your new back foot forward toward your target so that your feet are in the same position as when you started, only you'll be closer to your target. You can vary this technique by adding a kick to the end of it. To do this, bring your back foot over

Pivot Stepping
Begin in a fighting stance (left). Pivot on the back foot to move out of the way of a strike (right).

your front foot, then strike directly to the target with your back foot, using a side kick or a roundhouse kick.

Body Shifting

You can also practice evasive techniques by moving your body — body shifting — without moving your feet. This allows you to avoid a fighting technique while allowing you to set up a countering technique.

Timing Techniques

In sparring, timing is crucial. You need to be able to see an opening and strike immediately. But this is easier said than done. Usually by the time a fighter sees an opening and reacts, the opening is gone. By working on timing techniques, however, you'll be able to anticipate openings and react before they're gone. This is because each fighting technique has inherent strengths and weaknesses. Learning what these are and exploiting the weaknesses is the point of timing techniques. For example, the roundhouse kick is a good kick to use to reach someone's head. Its drawback is that it

Crossover Stepping
Begin in a fighting stance (above). Cross the back leg over the front leg (middle). Slide the new back leg forward toward the target (right).

Body Shifting
Use body shifting to avoid kicks and punches during sparring.

can leave your chest open. Therefore, if your partner performs a roundhouse kick, and you've been practicing your timing techniques, you will know to immediately throw a punch to your partner's chest, which is open and unblocked. The following timing technique drills will help you hone these skills. Remember to wear your safety equipment (also called sparring gear) when you are working on timing techniques. Although you should use care and control at all times, it is possible to make accidental contact, so sparring gear is essential.

Timing Technique Drills: Blocking

As you begin sparring, you will want to work on your ability to block your partner's techniques. By blocking the technique, you will avoid being struck. You can then move in with a technique of your own. Although several drills follow, you can devise your own, using kicking and blocking techniques that you devise yourself.

Punch Block

Work with a partner. Both of you should assume fighting stances. Have your partner punch to your middle section with his or her forward hand. Block this punch by performing a knife hand block with your forward hand. Practice until you are comfortable with actually knocking your partner's hand out of the way. Once you are, add a new element: block with your forward hand, then punch to your partner's middle section with your back hand. Add another punch with your forward hand. Kihop to show that you have finished, and return to your starting position.

Side Kick Block

Work with a partner. Both of you should assume fighting stances. Your chests should face the same direction. Have your partner kick with his or her front leg, using a side kick. You will respond by performing a low block to move your partner's leg out of the way. Your low block should be done with your forward hand, and you should block down over your forward leg. Once you understand the technique, go ahead and actually make the block, physically moving your partner's leg out of the way. As you do so, you will notice that your partner may let down his or her guard or might be slightly distracted or off-balance. This is exactly what you want. You will then step forward with your back leg and punch with your back hand. Kihop to show that you are done, then return to your starting position.

You should continue to practice this timing technique until you move quickly and smoothly, starting the block and punch as soon as you see the side kick coming. This is how you learn to anticipate openings and how you learn to start your countering technique before your opponent has even finished striking.

Front Kick Block

You can use the same technique to block a front kick out of the way. In this case, be sure to block downward to move the kick out of the way.

Reverse Kick Block

Work with a partner. Both of you should assume fighting stances. For this drill, your chests should face opposite directions. Have

(1)

(2)

(3)

(4)

Punch Block

Both partners assume fighting stances (1). As your partner punches, perform a knife hand block (2). Perform a punch to the partner's midsection (3). Perform another punch, this time to the high section (4).

your partner perform a reverse kick. Performing a low block with your forward arm, push the reverse kick out of the way. You will simply be pushing the kick in the same direction your partner is already rotating. Because you are using your partner's own momentum, the block is more of a pushing technique than a striking technique. Kihop to show that you are finished and return to your starting position.

Once you are comfortable pushing the reverse kick out of the way, add a punch by step-ping in with your back leg and punching to the middle section with your back hand.

Timing Technique Drills: Punching

As you grow more proficient with your timing techniques, you will no longer need to block the kicks and punches first before you counter them with your own attack. You will simply step, weave or duck out of the way and then

154

Side Kick Block
Your partner performs a side kick (left). Block the side kick away using a low block technique (right).

(1)

(3)

Block a Side Kick and Punch
Assume fighting stances (1). When your partner does a side kick, block it out of the way with a low block (2). Then step forward and punch (3).

(2)

155

Front Kick Block

Your partner performs a front kick (left). Perform a low block, striking down, to push the kick out of the way (right).

(1)

(2)

(3)

Punching Against a Side Kick

Your partner performs a side kick (1). Step to the side to avoid the kick (2). Step in and punch to your partner's midsection (3).

counter with a technique of your own. The best way to try this is to modify the timing techniques you have already been doing. Although several drills follow, you can devise your own, using kicking and blocking techniques that you devise yourself.

Punching Against a Side Kick

You and your partner should assume fighting stances, facing the same way. Have your partner perform a side kick with his or her for-

ward leg. Instead of blocking the kick, step to the side (stepping so that you are on the same side as your partner's chest). Then, step forward with your back leg and punch to the middle section with your back hand. Kihop to show that you are finished and return to the starting position.

Punching Against a Reverse Kick

You and your partner should assume fighting stances, facing in opposite directions. Have

(1)

Punching Against a Reverse Kick
Both partners assume fighting stances (1). Your partner performs a reverse kick (2). Step away from the kick (3). Punch to your partner's midsection with your back hand (4).

(2)

(3)

(4)

your partner perform a reverse kick. Instead of blocking the kick, take a step to the back to avoid the kick. Use a backward stepping technique: step back with your back foot, then step back with your front foot, so that you are still in the same stance facing the same direction; you have simply moved out of kicking range. Then step forward with your back leg and punch to the middle section with your back hand. Kihop to show that you are finished and return to the starting position.

Timing Technique Drills: Kicking

As you master the skills needed to perform blocking and punching timing techniques, you will start to learn the strengths and weaknesses of the different punches and kicks. This helps in two ways:

1. It helps you counter any techniques that a partner performs.
2. It helps you improve your techniques so that your weaknesses are harder to exploit.

For example, when your partner performs a reverse kick and you exploit the weakness (your partner's chest is unguarded and you can easily punch to it and score), you learn that when you perform a reverse kick, you should be careful to guard your chest. You can do this by making your hands into fists and keeping them up, covering your chest. This way, even if your opponent tries to counter with a punch, you will be ready to block the punch.

Once you understand the blocking and punching drills, you are ready to learn the timing techniques that allow you to counter a kick with a kick. This is a more difficult method of timing techniques, but it is also more successful, since you don't have to worry about blocking the technique out of the way and you don't have to move into punching range. Both blocking and punching require more time to execute than does using a kick to counter a kick.

Although several drills follow, you can devise your own, using timing techniques that you develop yourself.

(1)

(2)

(3)

Reverse Kick Against a Side Kick
Your partner performs a side kick (1). Rotate away from the kick (2). Perform a reverse kick (3).

Reverse Kick Against a Side Kick

Work with a partner. Assume fighting stances facing the opposite way. Have your partner perform a side kick using the front leg. As soon as you see your partner chamber the kick, immediately turn and perform a reverse kick, striking to your partner's middle section. Don't block the kick and then perform your technique. Simply by turning to do the reverse kick, you will avoid the side kick and you will take advantage of the opening that your partner's side kick has created. Kihop to show that you are finished and return to your starting position.

Reverse Kick Against a Reverse Kick

Work with a partner. Assume fighting stances facing opposite directions. Have your partner perform a reverse kick. As soon as your see your partner begin the reverse kick, perform a reverse kick of your own. Don't block your partner's kick first. By turning to do the reverse kick, you will avoid your partner's reverse kick and can take advantage of the opening that will be created. Kihop to show that you are finished and return to your starting position.

Reverse Kick Against Roundhouse Kick

Work with a partner. Assume fighting stances facing opposite directions. Have your partner perform a roundhouse kick with his or her back leg. As soon as your partner begins the roundhouse kick, perform a reverse kick. Don't block the roundhouse kick; by turning to do the reverse kick, you will avoid your partner's kick and can take advantage of the opening that will be created. Kihop to show that you are finished and return to your starting position.

Spinning Wheel Kick Against a Spinning Wheel Kick

Work with a partner. Assume fighting stances facing opposite directions. Have your partner perform a spinning wheel kick. As soon as you see your partner begin the spinning wheel kick, perform a spinning wheel kick of

(1)

(2)

(3)

Reverse Kick Against a Reverse Kick
Partners assume fighting stances (1). As your partner performs a reverse kick, turn away (2). Perform a reverse kick (3).

159

(1) (2)

Reverse Kick Against a Roundhouse Kick
Your partner performs a roundhouse kick (1). Perform a reverse kick as a counter (2).

your own. Don't block your partner's kick; by doing your own spinning wheel kick, you will avoid your partner's kick and can take advantage of the opening that will be created. Kihop to show that you are finished and return to your starting position.

Intermediate Timing Drills

Once you've become comfortable with the timing drills listed above, you can move on to more difficult timing technique drills. The best way to do this is to have both partners work on timing at the same time. For example, suppose your partner does a reverse kick. You know that a good timing technique to use to counter that kick is a reverse kick. So you perform a reverse kick. But then your partner sees your reverse kick coming and blocks it, following with a punch to your middle section. By combining several different drills, you and your partner can increase your skills and develop good freestyle sparring habits. Try putting together

(1) (2)

(3)

(4)

(5)

(6)

(7)

*Spinning Wheel Kick Against
a Spinning Wheel Kick*
Partners assume fighting stances (1, previous page). Partner begins a spinning wheel kick (2, previous page). Turn away from the kick to evade it (3). As your partner's kick is avoided, begin your own spinning wheel kick (4). Strike to your partner's head with the spinning wheel kick (5 and 6). Return to the starting position (7).

(1)

(2)

(3)

Intermediate Timing Drills
In this sequence, one partner performs a side kick that is blocked. But instead of allowing the other partner to counter, she adds a punch after her side kick.

(4)

the different drills listed above and add your own variations as you become more skilled.

Freestyle Sparring Drills

Working on timing techniques will help you learn to respond more quickly to openings by anticipating when those openings will occur. Timing techniques also help you see the strengths and weaknesses of each of the techniques that you use and will help you guard against the weaknesses.

However, martial artists frequently fall into a predictable routine when they spar. One partner will do a side kick. The other partner will do a reverse kick. The first partner will do a front kick. The other partner will do a punch. The fighters are only doing one or two techniques at a time, instead of trying to create openings by continuing to perform techniques. The more techniques you can perform in a row, the more likely you are to create an opening, distract your partner or overwhelm an oppo-

162

(1)

(3)

(2)

Intermediate Timing Drills
In this sequence, one partner performs a side kick (1). Her partner counters by performing a reverse kick (2), which she blocks and counters with a punch (3).

nent. To break this rhythm of one partner performing a technique then the other partner performing a technique, try practicing combination drills.

Combination Drills

Combination drills are designed to make you think about doing more than one or two techniques in a row. These drills help you understand how techniques flow and how to follow one technique with another. For example, if you perform a roundhouse kick and set your leg down so that you are in a horse stance position, you are at the perfect starting point to do a reverse kick. Therefore, a roundhouse kick–reverse kick combination can flow easily, without wasted effort. Or perhaps you are working on your spinning wheel kick. When you perform your spinning wheel kick, you still have some momentum helping you to rotate, so you can add a reverse kick. A spinning wheel–reverse kick combination is a good one. However, if you perform a front kick and then try to follow it with a spinning wheel kick, you won't have as much success. Combination drills help you understand the flow of techniques.

Combination Drill
As one partner moves
backward, the other
performs several tech-
niques in a row.

(1)

(2)

(3)

(4)

Basic Combination Drill

In the basic combination drill, you and your partner face each other in fighting stances. As you kihop, your partner moves backward so that you don't hit him or her with any of your techniques. Perform two techniques of any kind, and kihop to signal that you are through. Let your partner perform two techniques as you move backward. Then, perform three techniques of any kind, adding a kihop when you are finished. Have your partner perform three techniques. Continue adding one technique until you are doing five or six techniques in a row. Each time it is your turn to perform combinations of techniques, choose different techniques and put them in a different order. You and your partner can also discuss which techniques seemed to work well together and which did not.

Intermediate Combination Drills

As you become more proficient at combination drills, you will want to increase your speed so that you are performing your techniques quickly, just as if you were sparring.

To enhance your speed, try chasing your partner; that is, try to move quickly enough to land a technique even though your partner is moving back. Be certain to wear sparring equipment for this drill.

In addition, to work on combining techniques, have your partner call out a number from two to eight (or more, if you wish) before you begin your series of techniques. This is the number of techniques you must do in a row. Do the same for your partner. Call out a different number each time. This helps prevent you from falling into a predictable rhythm as you spar.

Partnerless Sparring Drills

Even if you don't have a partner, you can practice these drills yourself by imagining an opponent faces you and performing the techniques as directed. Although it is certainly more realistic to practice these drills with a partner, the lack of one should not keep you from practicing. In addition, sparring a heavy bag is an excellent workout and helps you string techniques together in a smooth attack sequence.

Sparring a heavy bag is an alternative to sparring with a partner.

The fighter practices sparring techniques without a partner in this series.

Freestyle Sparring Secrets

Even though sparring can seem intimidating at first — and actually getting kicked and punched can be disorienting, to say the least (plus it can hurt) — most martial artists who've been practicing a while say it is their favorite part of the workout. Give yourself time to learn the basics of freestyle sparring and begin by working with partners who agree to no contact. Go as slowly as you need at first, increasing your speed as you build confidence in yourself and your partner(s). You can also borrow a practice technique from boxing and try shadow sparring. To shadow spar, simply face a mirror and punch and kick the air, working on speed and striking combinations. Watch yourself in the mirror as you work. The important thing is to never let the lack of a partner stop you from practicing sparring.

Be Open to Learning

The key to freestyle sparring is realizing that there is always a lot more to learn. You can always become a better fighter by observation and critique. Spar with different partners and ask them to rate or discuss your performance. Some fighters have their sparring matches videotaped so that they can see what

their tendencies are and correct any weaknesses. Watch competitions to see what advanced fighters do. Read instructional articles and books and watch how-to videos. Most of all, practice on your own.

Mental Preparation

Keep in mind that much of sparring is mental rather than physical. If you have confidence in yourself as you spar, you are more likely to react quickly and without hesitation. If you are unsure of yourself, you may let opportunities to score pass you by. Especially at first it can be difficult to develop confidence, since you aren't sure what you're doing. That's why practicing timing techniques and combination drills is so important — these help to prepare you for the real thing.

Stay Focused

It's important not to get distracted from sparring by discouragement or frustration. Even if your partner is scoring points and you are unable to get past his or her guard, you have to continue fighting confidently. If you let your doubts influence you, your opponent will have won without scoring a point. Therefore, your attitude is essential to good sparring. Realize that even bad sparring experiences help you learn and grow as a martial artist.

Remember, too, that some people enjoy playing mental games with others. They'll try and distract you by talking or doing flashy kicks or otherwise provoking you. Don't be touched by this. If you show that you are undisturbed by another fighter's antics, pretty soon he or she will stop trying.

Finally, always look your opponent in the eye as you spar. This is fundamental but hard to do. Don't watch your partner's arms and legs to see what kicks or punches might be coming at you. Learn to respond instinctively as you sense a strike coming. Keeping your eyes up sends a message of confidence and also helps keep you from getting distracted and falling for feints.

Worry Only About Yourself

Concern yourself only with what you are doing. Worry only about your own sparring. Are you taking advantage of openings that come up? Are you anticipating your partner's techniques? Are you getting faster, stronger, smarter? Don't concern yourself with how you compare to your partner or to other martial artists. Learn to be the best martial artist you can be. The true competition is yourself. Just look your opponent in the eye and go for it.

Size up Your Opponent

Although you want to only worry about yourself, you do have to consider your opponent since you are, after all, sparring him or her. Before you consider your opponent, though, ask yourself some questions. Do you spar hard hitters the same way you spar light contact fighters? Do you spar tall people the same way you spar short ones? You shouldn't. If your opponent favors fast-paced, aggressive attacks, you won't be successful treating him or her the way you do someone who relies on countering techniques. You can't let your opponent control the match but you should take his or her sparring tactics into consideration when planning your own strategy.

Add Variety to Your Sparring

All martial artists have some techniques that work especially well for them. For one, it might be a spinning wheel kick. For another, it might be a backfist. Frequently, fighters start to rely on a select few tried-and-true techniques. While this makes sparring easier because it is more automatic, it also makes it less challenging and ultimately less successful. By adding variety to your sparring repertoire, you'll improve your martial arts skills, confound your opponents and increase your self-confidence. Remaining unpredictable is essential to sparring.

Try this: instead of using one technique that you like, replace it with another one that you don't use very often. Every time you plan to use your favored technique, use the new one instead. For example, suppose you like to use a reverse kick when you spar. Plan to use a spinning wheel kick instead. Every time you start to use your reverse kick, turn it into a spinning wheel kick. Although this may slow you down slightly at first, the change is worth the effort. Even if you have practiced your reverse kick as a countering technique, the spinning wheel kick will be just as effective. Once you've forced yourself to add the spinning wheel kick, you can continue to use the reverse kick — just not so frequently.

Feinting

As you grow more skilled at sparring, you can learn to set up scoring opportunities by feinting. This means pretending to do a certain technique but stopping before you are committed to it, in order to make your partner respond. (This is what a boxer uses a jab for.) Using a feinting technique will allow you to create openings that you can then respond to. For example, suppose you begin a side kick by drawing your leg up to the chamber position and extending it slightly. Your partner may try to counter the side kick he or she sees by blocking it or by doing a reverse kick as a counter. By stopping your technique — feinting — you can get your partner to block or kick. Once your partner is committed to the technique, you can counter by performing a technique of your own to an unguarded area, such as your partner's head.

You could feint a side kick, wait until your partner leaned forward to block and then, while your opponent's hands and mind are occupied with the block, perform a roundhouse kick to the head. Feints can be used with any technique and can greatly improve your sparring practice.

Learn from Your Mistakes

Perhaps the most difficult aspect of martial arts training is trying to learn from your mistakes. It is easy to see that your side kick gets blocked all the time, but it is not so easy to see how this can change. That's why you should get in the habit of talking with your sparring partners on a regular basis. If they see you perform techniques that don't work or that they repeatedly counter, they can tell you. They can also give tips on how to fix that.

You will also need to spend time analyzing your sparring and considering how to improve. If every time you do a reverse kick your partner avoids it and counters with a reverse punch, ask yourself what you can change, other than never doing the reverse kick again. Perhaps you could do a reverse kick that only goes 180 degrees instead of a full 360 degrees. This might confuse your partner and make the reverse punch ineffective. Or follow your first reverse kick quickly with a second reverse kick, which makes an excellent counter to a punch. Experiment with these changes and then incorporate them into your sparring.

Find Your Strengths

Finding your strengths requires that you be completely honest with yourself. Take a look at your body type. Are you tall, short or medium? Are you big or little or somewhere in between? Do you have especially long arms or legs? These questions can help you determine which techniques are best for you.

Make an honest assessment of your inherent physical abilities (not your Tae Kwon Do skills). Are you quick? Agile? Powerful? Flexible? Pick techniques that complement your abilities.

Consider the Tae Kwon Do techniques you know, and list those that work best for you. Think about changes you can make by finding the strengths in this assessment. For example, if you are especially short, you may not think that's much of a strength. It's hard to kick taller people head high when you're short. If you're also little, it's hard to perform with power, and how can that be a strength?

But it's simply a matter of perspective. A small, light person can be agile, which means he or she can move into and out of fighting ranges quickly and can use countering or timing techniques better than bigger, more powerful people. A small, light person can also spar in close, using the punching range. This is disorienting to taller people who are used to having an advantage in kicking range. Also, quicker is better in sparring; you can react to openings more easily than bigger, slower people.

But don't limit yourself to one-dimensional fighting. Even if you are small and light, you can improve your strength and power. If you are big and powerful, you can work on your flexibility and speed. Success in sparring, as in Tae Kwon Do itself, is a matter of seeing it as an ongoing process, not a result at which you will one day arrive and never have to change.

Condition for Sparring

In order to spar to the best of your ability, you should condition yourself. Flexibility training, speed training and power training are all important elements to your success as a fighter. Eating right, getting enough rest and treating your body well are also essential to excellence in martial arts. See Part VI for drills to improve your flexibility, speed and power.

Part IV

19

The Philosophy of Self-Defense

Most people begin martial arts training at least in part because they wish to learn self-defense, hoping it will help them should they ever face a physical confrontation. In Tae Kwon Do, self-defense techniques and philosophy are begun very early in training.

Tae Kwon Do as a Defensive Skill

The techniques of Tae Kwon Do are meant to be used for two reasons:

1. Achievement of a better-balanced life
2. Self-defense

Sparring, forms practice, conditioning and other elements of Tae Kwon Do training are fun and challenging, and they provide benefits that range from improved fitness to better self-confidence. But what underlies all practice is the belief that you learn these skills to defend yourself. A Tae Kwon Do practitioner should never, under any circumstances, misuse his or her skills by instigating a fight or otherwise acting aggressively. If a tense situation develops, the Tae Kwon Do practitioner is expected to use reason, either by calmly discussing the matter or by walking away. A Tae Kwon Do practitioner never throws the first punch. He or she must always insist, "I don't want to fight."

When to Use Tae Kwon Do

Only if your wishes are disregarded and you are in peril of being physically injured should you use Tae Kwon Do techniques against another person. Do the smart thing. Hand over your wallet if someone demands it. Walk away if someone calls you a name. Don't use kicks and punches unless you have no alternative. Be aware that even if someone else starts the fight, you can be charged with assault and other crimes if you overreact. People who study fighting skills, such as martial artists and boxers, are often held to a higher standard than people who have not studied fighting techniques. Be very judicious when using your martial arts skills.

The Three Levels of Defense

In Tae Kwon Do, self-defense is thought to have three levels or stages. The first is the escape level. In this case, you simply attempt to escape from the attacker without injury to yourself or your attacker. The second is control. In this case, you stop the attacker by controlling his or her body. Although a control technique might cause some temporary discomfort, it does not cause any permanent harm. The third level is the counter level and is only used when the previous two levels have failed to convince the attacker to stop the harassment. In this case, you will counter with a technique that will inflict physical damage on your attacker. Level three techniques should never be used in response to minor attacks such as someone grabbing your shirt.

Finish the Fight

Most Tae Kwon Do self-defense techniques have been developed so that they can begin at stage one and move through stages two and three if needed. That is, each technique gives you the option of escaping, controlling or countering your attacker.

Remember that once you have begun using physical means to deter an attacker, you must be committed to winning the fight. This doesn't mean you have to destroy your attacker, it simply means you must be ready to do whatever it takes to end the fight or get away from the attacker. Don't throw a punch unless you mean to make it hurt. If you aren't committed to winning the fight, you should not be using physical means of resistance. Martial artists often call this "finishing" the fight or "finishing" the opponent.

Don't make a half-hearted attempt to perform a knife hand strike to an attacker unless you simply want to make him or her angry. Either perform the technique appropriately and with confidence, or do not do it at all. If you've committed to one kick, you must be willing to execute another if the first one doesn't stop your attacker. This sort of preparedness is necessary to effective self-defense.

Joint Locks

Tae Kwon Do teaches the use of joint locks in self-defense. Joint locks are methods for immobilizing an opponent by manipulating his or her joints, usually by pushing or pulling the joint in the direction opposite to its natural movement. Locks can be applied to any joint. They work as a method of controlling the opponent without causing permanent physical harm.

Vital Point Strikes

Attacking the vital points of the body can be devastating to the attacker, since these are the most vulnerable parts of the body. These are usually level three techniques because they are meant to cause physical harm to the opponent. Vital points vulnerable to strikes include the following:

- Eye
- Inner wrist
- Temple
- Solar plexus
- Ear
- Floating ribs
- Nose
- Small of back
- Jaw
- Kidney
- Throat
- Tailbone
- Side of neck
- Groin
- Shoulder blade
- Knee
- Armpit
- Achilles heel
- Elbow
- Instep

Vital point strikes can be used along with joint locks if the joint lock alone is not sufficient to stop the attacker.

Armed Attackers

The techniques described in this section are for use in a confrontation in which both participants are unarmed. Although there are self-defense techniques that work against armed attackers, these are advanced techniques and require special training. If someone intends to harm you and is armed, you must decide to what extent you can and will fight. If the attacker is likely to leave you alone if you give up your wallet, then by all means you should do so. On the other hand, if the attacker seems certain to harm you, then by all means you should fight. It is best to think about self-defense scenarios ahead of time, although you never know how you will react when under pressure. But by thinking ahead, if you ever find yourself facing an armed attacker, you will have already decided what route you want to take. If you believe that submitting will cause the least amount of harm to you, then, having decided that, accept it. But if you think an attacker is more likely to hurt you if you don't put up a fight, then be prepared to fight. Only you can decide which is the right course of action for you to take.

Weapons

People often purchase weapons, usually guns, for the purpose of protecting themselves, their loved ones and their property. Tragically, guns and other weapons often end up injuring and killing innocent bystanders. If you choose to keep a weapon, you must be sure it is safe, so that children or others do not accidentally shoot themselves or someone else. You must also be responsible enough to see that your weapon is never used for anything but the most serious of dangerous situations. Unfortunately, weapons are often used to intimidate family members and friends during disagreements, with disastrous results. Finally, you must be willing to learn how to use the weapon, and you must be willing to use it. Although it might seem a simple matter to aim a gun and shoot it, the matter is not so simple. Invest in lessons at a firing range. As with all skills, weapons use requires constant practice. You must also ask yourself if you could really use a weapon against another person. This is another reason why lessons are good. They can help you see what shooting a target feels like. You must imagine what this would feel like and then be convinced that you can do it. Otherwise, it is too easy for your own weapon to be used against you. In general, weapons such as guns and knives are a danger to individuals and society at large and conscientious martial artists should avoid them.

Environmental Weapons

This is not to say that there aren't times when a weapon might be appropriate to use. But if you need additional help in fending off an attacker, your best bet is an environmental weapon. There are two reasons for this.

1. An environmental weapon is not likely to harm an innocent bystander, and even if you use it against an attacker, it is unlikely to actually cause death. Using excessive force even against a person with obvious criminal intentions can land you in jail.

2. Environmental weapons are all around us and readily available, unlike other weapons. Unless that .45 is strapped to your thigh at all times, you can easily be caught unaware. The weapon you invested in will be useless if it's sitting in the dresser drawer and you're car-jacked on the way home from work.

Environmental weapons include any object that can be used to strike or poke a person. The telephone in your hand can add power to a strike. The pencil over your ear could be poked in someone's eye. Environmental weapons are also objects that can be thrown at an attacker. If you used to pitch for your high school baseball team, your child's softball could be thrown at an attacker.

Look around your home, school, office and other areas where you spend time. How many weapons do you see and how could you use them if you needed to?

20

Basic and Intermediate Self-Defense Techniques

Tae Kwon Do teaches self-defense techniques to use in common or typical scenarios, such as when someone grabs your arm or sleeve and threatens you. By practicing set responses, you can feel more confident that you'll respond quickly and appropriately to an attack.

Working with a partner, practice the self-defense techniques listed below. As you become more comfortable with what you are doing, you can add your own techniques and ideas, tailoring your techniques to your own skills. When practicing, be sure both partners kihop before starting so that no accidental injuries occur. Instead of assuming a fighting stance, as you do for most drills, approach these more naturally, as if you were going about your ordinary business. The self-defense techniques described are used in response to specific kinds of attacks. If someone grabs your wrist, there is a specific self-defense technique. If someone grabs your sleeve, there is a specific self-defense technique. Practice these until they become second nature; then, if someone were to grab your wrist or your sleeve, you would be able to respond without hesitation. For some kinds of attacks, there are several possible defenses. These are given in order from least to most difficult. Work on all

of them, learning how they are properly performed, before deciding which of them works best for you. All self-defense techniques shown begin with the level one technique, that is, the technique that will allow you to escape. Level two and level three techniques are then shown as variations.

Attacks from the Front

Against a Wrist Grab

Level One

Work with a partner. Face the same way. Have your partner grab your left wrist with his or her right hand. Twist your hand away, pulling sharply.

Level Two

There are several variations for Level Two.

1. When your partner grabs your right wrist, grip it with your left hand. Peel your partner's hand away, twisting the arm in an arc. Continue to twist your partner's hand to control it.

2. When your partner grabs your right wrist, grip it with your left hand. Turn to your right while stepping away from your partner. Pull

175

Self-Defense Against a Wrist Grab

Level 1
Your partner grabs your wrist (left). Twist away, pulling your hand free (right).

(1)   (2)   (3)

Level Two, Variation 1

Grasp your partner's hand (1). Peel your partner's hand away, twisting his arm in an arc (2). Continue to twist your partner's hand to control it (3).

(1)   (2)   (3)   (4)

Level Two, Variation 2

When your partner grabs your wrist, cover his hand with your free hand (1). Swing your arm, stepping away (2). Turn away from your partner, lifting the arm high (3). Pull your partner's arm down, striking his or her elbow against your shoulder (4).

Self-Defense Against a Wrist Grab

Level Three, Variation 1
Your partner grabs your wrist (left). Deliver a side kick to the ribs (right).

(1) (2) (3)

Level Three, Variation 2
Your partner grabs your wrist (1). Pull free (2) and deliver a backfist strike to your partner's temple (3).

your partner's arm over your shoulder with his palm facing up. When your partner's elbow rests on your shoulder, pull downward.

Level Three

There are several variations for Level Three.

1. When your partner grabs your left wrist with his or her right hand, lean backward and deliver a left leg sidekick to your partner's ribs.

2. When your partner grabs your left wrist, pull free and strike to the temple with a back fist.

Against a Two-Wrist Grab

Level One

Working with a partner, both facing the same way, have your partner grab both of your wrists. Swing your arms upward, putting your hands into the knife hand position. Push down on your partner's wrists to force him or her to release you. Push your partner away while stepping back.

Level Two

Have your partner grab your wrists. Pull one hand free, as you would for a single

Self-Defense Against a Two-Wrist Grab

(1)

(2)

(3)

Level One
Your partner grabs both wrists (1). Swing your arms upward (2) and make your hands into knife hands (3). Press down on your partner's hands until he releases you (4).

(4)

Self-Defense Against a Two-Wrist Grab

(1)　　　　　　(2)　　　　　　(3)

Level Two

Pull one wrist free, as for a single wrist grab (1). With your free hand, grasp your partner's hand (2). Turn and press your elbow against your partner's elbow to create an arm lock (3).

wrist grab. With your free hand, trap your partner's other hand. Turn away from your partner and press the point of your elbow against your partner's elbow to create an arm lock.

Level Three

When your partner grabs both of your wrists, swing your arms up and twist your hands, pulling free. Perform a front kick to your partner's midsection or groin.

(1)　　　　　(2)

(3)

(4)

Level Three

After your partner grabs both wrists, swing your arms up (1). Pull your wrists free (2). Deliver a front kick to the groin or midsection (3, 4).

Self-Defense Against a Sleeve Grab

(1)　(2)　(3)

Level One
Your partner grabs your sleeve above the elbow (1). With your free hand, perform a palm strike to escape (2 and 3).

(1)　(2)　Level Two　(3)

Your partner grabs your sleeve (1). Swing your arm up (2). Wrap your arm around your partner's arm (3). Press your forearm against your partner's arm to exert control (4).

(4)

Against a Sleeve Grab

Level One

Working with a partner, facing each other, have your partner grab your sleeve or upper arm. With your free hand, perform a palm strike to your partner's arm to knock his or her grasp loose.

Level Two

When you partner grabs your sleeve, raise your arm and wrap it around your partner's arm just above the elbow. Twist and lift to gain control of your partner.

Self-Defense Against a Sleeve Grab

(1)

(2)

(3)

(4)

Level Three

Perform an arm wrap (1 and 2). Then deliver a roundhouse kick to your partner's midsection (3). As a variation, perform an uppercut to your partner's exposed ribs (4).

Level Three

When you partner grabs your sleeve, raise your arm and wrap it around your partner's arm just above the elbow. Then deliver a roundhouse kick to your partner's midsection. Or, step forward, and with your free hand, strike to your partner's exposed ribs.

181

Self-Defense Against a Shirt/Lapel Grab

(1)   (2)   (3)

Level One

Your partner grasps your shirt or lapel from the front (1). With your nearest hand, perform a palm strike to your partner's arm (2 and 3).

(1)   (2)   (3)

(4)   (5)

Level Two

Your partner grabs your lapel (1). Reach over and peel your partner's hand away (2). Using both hands, twist your partner's hand (3). The partner's arm and palm should face upward (4). Continue twisting to keep control (5).

Self-Defense Against a Shirt/Lapel Grab

(1) (2) (3)

Level Three
When your partner grabs your lapel, peel his hand off (1). Grab your partner's elbow (2). Throw your partner to the ground (3).

Against a Shirt/Lapel Grab

Level One

Working with a partner, facing each other, have your partner grab your shirt or jacket from the front. With your nearest hand, perform a palm strike to your partner's arm to knock his or her grasp away.

Level Two

When your partner grabs your shirt or jacket, grasp your partner's hand with your nearest hand, peeling your partner's hand away. With both hands, twist your partner's hand over so that his or her palm and elbow are facing upward. Continue twisting to keep control.

Level Three

When your partner grabs your shirt or jacket, grasp your partner's hand and peel it away. With your free hand, push your partner's elbow up in order to upset his or her balance. Slide your foot behind your partner's foot and throw your partner backward.

Against a Choke Hold

Level One

There are several variations for this.

1. When your partner performs the choke hold, push away his or her right arm by performing a palm strike to it with your right hand. Push away his or her left arm by performing a palm strike to it with your left hand. This releases your partner's grip so you can escape.

2. Working with your partner, facing each other, have your partner grab your throat with both hands. Lift both arms up over your head, turn quickly and escape. A counter can be added by simply performing a side kick once free. (This is a Level Three response.)

Level Two

When your partner performs the chokehold, raise one arm. Turn toward your partner, trapping his or her arms. This releases the hold and controls your partner. As a counter, add an elbow strike at the end. (This is a Level Three response.)

Self-Defense Against a Choke Hold

(1)

(2) **Level One, Variation 1**

(3)

Your partner performs a choke hold (1). Perform a palm strike to your partner's arm (2). Perform another palm strike to the other arm (3).

Level Three

When your partner performs the chokehold, strike to both sides of your partner's body with knife hands. This helps loosen your partner's hold. Then slide your arms up between his arms and spread your arms. As your partner releases his hold, strike to his or her neck with both hands. Then grab your partner's neck and pull him or her down. Drive a knee strike into your partner's chest.

Attacks from Behind

Attacks from behind are more difficult to defend against because they are usually unexpected. Once you have practiced and learned the basic self-defense techniques for attacks from the front, go on to attacks from the back. Use the following examples to start. Then, as you become proficient, add your own variations and techniques.

Against Two-Wrist Grab from Behind

Level One

Work with a partner. Have your partner grab both of your wrists from behind. Step to the side and twist sharply toward your partner. When your partner releases your hands, escape.

Level Two

When your partner grabs your wrists, step backward and raise your outside arm (and, therefore, your partner's arm.) Lower your body and slide under your partner's arm. Stand up. Twist your partner's arm behind his back to control it.

Level Three

There are several variations for Level Three:

1. When your partner grabs your wrists, step forward or back to move into kicking range. Kick straight back with your heel, aiming for the groin or solar plexus.

2. When your partner grabs your wrists, step backward while raising your outer arm (and, therefore, your partner's arm.) Lower your body and slide under your partner's arm. Stand up. Push down with your hands to control your partner's hands. Follow with a knee strike to your partner's solar plexus.

Self-Defense Against a Choke Hold

(1)

(2)

Level One, Variation 2
Lift your arms above your head (1). Turn, breaking your partner's grip. Step free (2). To counter, add a side kick (3). Adding a kick makes this a Level Three response.

(3)

Self-Defense Against a Choke Hold

(1) (2) (3)

Level Two

After your partner performs a choke hold, raise one arm (1). Turn toward your partner, bringing your arm down and trapping his hands (2). This can be turned into a Level Three response by adding an elbow strike (3).

(1) (2) (3) (4)

Level Three

When your partner performs a choke hold, perform knife hand strikes to both sides of his chest (1). Slide your arms up between your partner's arms (2) and grab his neck (3). Pull your partner down while delivering a knee strike (4).

Self-Defense Against a Two-Wrist Grab from Behind

(1)

(2)

(3)

(4)

Level One
Your partner grabs both wrists from behind (1). Step to the side (2) and turn sharply toward your partner (3). Slide away from your partner (4).

Self-Defense Against a Two-Wrist Grab from Behind

(1)　　　　(2)　　　　(3)　　　　(4)

Level Two

Your partner grabs both wrists from behind (1). Step backward while raising your outside arm (2). Lower your body and slide under your partner's arm (3). Stand up. Twist your partner's arm to control it (4).

Level Three, Variation 1 (Above)

When your partner grabs your wrists, kick straight back, aiming for the midsection or groin.

Level Three, Variation 2 (Right)

Your partner grabs both wrists from behind (1). Step backward while raising your outside arm (2). Slide under your partner's arm and stand up (3). Deliver a knee strike to the midsection (4).

(1)　　　　(2)

(3)　　　　(4)

Against a Sleeve Grab from Behind

Level One

Work with a partner. Have your partner grab your sleeve from behind. Turn toward your partner, striking his or her arm with a palm strike. Knock your partner's arm away.

Level Two

When your partner grabs your sleeve, turn toward him or her, making your hand a knife hand. Grab your partner's wrist and shoulder. Twist your partner's wrist and press down on his or her shoulder. Continue pressing to control your partner. Add a roundhouse kick as a counter. (This is a Level Three response.)

Level Three

When your partner grabs your sleeve from behind, perform an elbow strike with your free arm, aiming for your partner's solar plexus. Then turn slightly and perform a backfist to your partner's face.

Self-Defense Against a Sleeve Grab from Behind

(1)

(2)

(3)

(4)

Level One
Your partner grabs your sleeve from behind (1). Turn toward your partner's arm (2), then use a palm strike to knock your partner's hand away (3, 4).

Self-Defense Against a Sleeve Grab from Behind

(1)

(2)

(3)

(4)

(5)

(6)

Level Two

Your partner grabs your sleeve from behind *(1)*. Turn toward your partner *(2)* and grab his wrist and shoulder *(3)*. Twist his wrist while pressing down on his shoulder *(4)*. Continue twisting to control your partner *(5)*. Turn the technique into a Level Three response by adding a roundhouse kick to the midsection *(6)*.

(1)   *(2)*   *(3)*

Level Three

As your partner grabs your sleeve from behind, chamber for an elbow strike *(1)*. Perform an elbow strike to your partner's midsection *(2)*, then perform a backfist to his face *(3)*.

Self-Defense Against a One-Arm Chokehold from Behind

(1)

(2)

(3)

Level One, Variation 1
Your partner performs a one-arm chokehold from behind (1). Turn toward your partner and lean forward (2). Keep turning and pull free (3).

Against a One-Arm Chokehold from Behind

Level One

1. Work with a partner. Have your partner grab you in a one-arm chokehold from behind.

Turn so that your throat rests in the crook of your partner's elbow. This ensures that you will be able to breathe even if your partner tightens the chokehold. Turn toward your partner and lean forward. Keep turning and pull your head free.

(1)

(2)

(3)

Level One, Variation 2
Your partner performs a chokehold (1). Turn toward your partner and lean down. Reach up and claw his face (2). Push your partner backward until the chokehold is released (3).

Self-Defense Against a One-Arm Chokehold from Behind

2. Have your partner perform a chokehold. Turn toward your partner and lean down. Reach up and claw at your partner's face. Push your partner backward to force him or her to release you.

Level Two

As your partner chokes you from behind, turn so that your throat rests in the crook of your partner's elbow. This ensures that you will be able to breathe even if your partner tight-ens the chokehold. Turn toward your partner and lean down. Reach up and grab the wrist of your partner's choking arm. Pull free, holding onto partner's wrist. Twist your partner's arm behind his or her back. Continue twisting to control your partner.

Level Three

As your partner chokes you from behind, turn so that your throat rests in the crook of your partner's elbow, ensuring that you will be

(1)

(2)

(3)

(4)

(5)

Level Two
Your partner performs a chokehold (1). Turn toward your partner and lean down. Grab the wrist of his choking arm (2). Pull free, holding onto his arm (3). Twist your partner's arm behind his back (4). Continue twisting to control your partner (5).

Self-Defense Against a One-Arm Chokehold from Behind

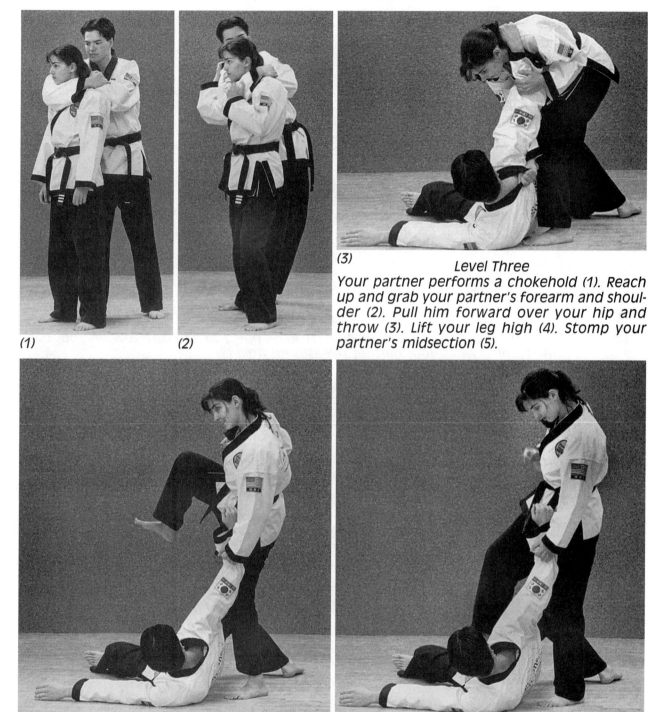

(1) *(2)* *(3)* *(4)* *(5)*

Level Three
Your partner performs a chokehold (1). Reach up and grab your partner's forearm and shoulder (2). Pull him forward over your hip and throw (3). Lift your leg high (4). Stomp your partner's midsection (5).

able to breathe even if your partner tightens the chokehold. Reach behind you and grab your partner's shirt, hair or upper arm. Keep turning and pull down on your partner's arm to disrupt his balance. Throw your partner to the ground, then finish with a stomp to your partner's ribs.

Against a Two-Handed Chokehold from Behind
Level One

Work with a partner. Have your partner grasp your throat with both hands. Raise one arm and turn toward your raised arm. Keep turning until you break your partner's grip.

Self-Defense Against a Two-Handed Chokehold from Behind

(1) (2) (3)

Level One

Your partner performs a two-handed chokehold (1). Raise one arm and turn toward your partner (2). Continue turning while your partner releases his hold (3).

(1) (2) (3)

(4)

Level Two

Your partner performs a chokehold (1). Grab your partner's hands (2). Step and turn away from your partner. Lean forward (3). Pull free. Press your partner's wrist forward to control his arm (4).

Self-Defense Against a Two-Handed Chokehold from Behind

Level Three
When your partner peforms a chokehold, raise one arm and turn toward your partner (1). Deliver a palm strike to your partner's face (2).

(1)   (2)

Level Two

When your partner grasps your throat, rise up on the balls of your feet. Reach back and cover your partner's hands with your palms. Step away from your partner, turn and lean forward. Continue gripping your partner's wrist to control his or her arm.

Level Three

When your partner grasps your throat, raise one arm. Turn toward your raised arm. Keep turning until you break your partner's grip. Then follow with a palm strike to your partner's face.

Secrets of Self-Defense

The key to effective self-defense is continual practice. This allows you to respond quickly to a threat. As in other areas of Tae Kwon Do, acting with confidence is essential. Further, it is important to be committed to winning the fight. This means using as many techniques as necessary.

Also, think through possible self-defense scenarios ahead of time to help prepare. Consider where you spend your time, what you like to do and what you wear. If you're a woman who wears skirts and heels to work everyday, you must think about this and realize that you

might not be able to do certain kicking techniques without losing your balance (try doing a spinning wheel kick in high heels!). By the same token, however, you could drive the heel of one of your shoes into an attacker's instep and cause an awful lot of pain. As you go through your daily activities, stop and think about how you could defend against an attacker given the exact circumstances that are around you. If you can't think of a self-defense technique that might work, spend some time during your Tae Kwon Do workout to arrive at a solution to the problem.

Consider what to do in different self-defense scenarios.

(1)

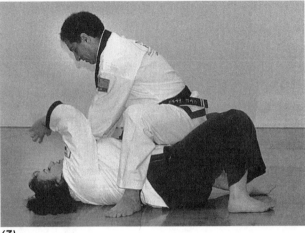

(3)

Practice self-defense techniques from a variety of positions.

(2)

(4)

Use environmental weapons in self-defense.

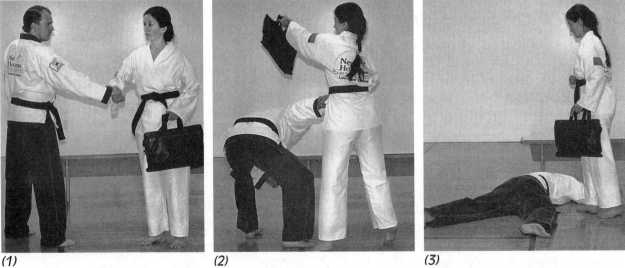

(1)   (2)   (3)

Use environmental weapons in self-defense.

(1)

(2)

(3)

(1)

(2)

(3)

Part V

21

Chon-ji Form

Forms are an essential part of martial arts practice. In Korean, a form is called a *hyung*. A form is a pattern of prearranged movements that a student must memorize and perform with grace, balance and power. Not only does the form showcase the student's techniques, it also teaches him or her how to put techniques together in an artful way. Forms are also a good way to practice martial arts techniques in a small amount of space, and to learn focus and concentration. At the higher black belt ranks, students are expected to make up their own martial arts forms.

In Tae Kwon Do, a new form is taught at each belt level. Some schools require their students to learn more than one form at each belt level. These forms must be memorized; the student should be able to do any form he or she has ever learned at any time. This requires continual practice.

Symbolic Value of Forms

Tae Kwon Do forms have a symbolic aspect. Often, they are named after important people in Korean history. The shape of a pattern may refer to an ideogram — that is, a written character that stands for a Korean word. The number of movements in a form may have special significance. This is so students will learn a little about Korean past and tradition as they learn their forms.

The Meaning of *Chon-ji* Hyung

Chon-ji form is the first form a Tae Kwon Do student is taught. The name means "heaven and earth." In Korea, this is interpreted to refer to the beginning of both the world and human history. For this reason, it is the beginner form. There are two parts to the pattern; one represents heaven and the other, earth. There are 19 techniques. Each should be performed with equal power, balance, agility and grace.

Chon-ji Hyung

The form makes a cross pattern. To perform it, you must assume that four opponents are challenging you, one from the front, one from the back and one from each of the sides. The techniques used are the ready stance, a low block in a front stance, a straight punch in a front stance and an inside-outside crescent block in a back stance.

(1)

(2)

Low Block in Front Stance
Start in a chunbee stance (1). Look toward the target and chamber your blocking hand on your opposite shoulder (2). Step into the new front stance position (3). Sweep the blocking arm down (4). Twist your wrist so that the palm faces down. The block should stop just beyond the forward knee (5).

(3)   (4)   (5)

(1)

(2)

(3)

(4)

(5)

Punch in Front Stance
Begin in a blocking position (1). Bring the back foot in (2). Step forward and begin punch (3). Continue stepping and punching (4). Finish in a new front stance. Your wrist should twist so that the palm faces down as the punch strikes (5).

(1)   (2)   (3)   (4)

Inside-Outside Crescent Block in Back Stance
From the punching position, chamber the blocking hand under the arm (1). Step in to the back stance while sweeping the blocking arm outward (2). Continue sweeping (3). As the block lands, twist the wrist so the palm faces in. The block should be done in a strong back stance (4).

Begin Part I

Begin in the ready stance (left). Look to the left to see your first attacker. Note: Most movements in parts 1 and 2 are illustrated by two photos depicting the same movement from two angles.

Movement 1

Step and turn to the left with your left leg, moving into a front stance with your left leg forward. As you move, low block with your left arm over your left leg.

Movement 2

Then, step forward with your right leg, moving into a front stance. At the same time, perform a straight punch to the middle section with your right hand. You should be in a strong front stance, your arm extended. Do not drop your punch. Keep your eyes forward; do not look around.

Movement 3

Turn and step 180 degrees to your right, moving into a front stance with your right leg forward. As you move, perform a low block with your right arm over your right leg.

Movement 4

Step forward with your left leg, moving into a front stance. At the same time, perform a straight punch to the middle section with your left hand. You should be in a strong front stance, your arm extended. Again, do not drop your punch and keep your eyes forward.

Movement 5 (left)

Pick up your left leg and turn 90 degrees. You should be in a strong front stance, facing the same direction as when you started. As you move, low block over your left leg.

Movement 6 (right)

Step forward with your right leg, moving into a front stance. As you move, perform a straight punch to the middle section with your right hand. You should be in a strong front stance, your arm extended, your eyes forward.

Movement 7

Turn and step 180 degrees to the right. You should be in a strong front stance. As you move, perform a low block with your right arm over your right leg.

Movement 8

Step forward with your left leg, moving into a front stance. As you move, perform a straight punch to the middle section with your left hand. You should be in a strong front stance, your arm extended, your eyes forward.

End of Part I

You have finished the first part of the pattern. You may wish to repeat it several times before going on to the second part if it is easier for you to learn by breaking it into smaller pieces.

Begin Part II

The second part of the pattern begins here. You should be/remain in the same position as at the end of Part I.

Movement 9

Step and turn with your left leg, moving 90 degrees. This time you should be in a back stance, with most of the weight on your back leg. As you turn, perform an inside-outside crescent block with your left arm.

Movement 10

Stepping forward with your right leg, perform a straight punch to the middle section. You should be in a strong front stance, your arm extended, your eyes forward.

Movement 11

Turn and step right 180 degrees, performing an inside-outside block with your right arm as you turn. You should be in a good back stance.

Movement 12

Step forward with your left leg and perform a straight punch to the middle section. You should be in a strong front stance, your arm extended, eyes forward.

Movement 13

Turn and step left 90 degrees, performing an inside-outside block with your left arm as you turn. You should be in a good back stance.

Movement 14

Step forward with your right leg and perform a straight punch to the middle section. You should be in a strong front stance, your arm extended, eyes forward.

Movement 15 (left)

Turn and step right 180 degrees, until you are facing the position in which you started the form. Perform an inside-outside block as you move. You should be in a strong back stance.

Movement 16 (right)

Step forward with your left leg and perform a straight punch to the middle section. You should be in a strong front stance, your arm extended, eyes forward.

Movement 17

Then, step forward with your right leg, punching with your right hand to the middle section as you go. You should be in a strong front stance.

Movement 18

Next, step back with your right leg, punching with your left hand to the middle section as you go. You should be in a strong front stance with your left leg forward and your left hand extended.

Movement 19

Finally, step back with your left leg, punching with your right hand to the middle section as you go. You should end in a strong front stance with your right leg forward and your right hand extended. Kihop loudly as you finish the form.

Part VI

22

Flexibility Drills

Flexibility is needed to perform many Tae Kwon Do techniques, especially the high kicks and the jumping kicks. A number of stretching exercises can improve flexibility, especially the hip/groin stretch, the back stretch, and the hamstring stretch as described in Part II, Chapter 6.

In addition, the following flexibility exercises will improve your ability to kick.

Side Bends
Standing straight up, tilt to the side, reaching up and over your head. Hold for 15 seconds.

Side Bend

Standing up straight, tilt your upper body to the side, reaching over the top of your head with the opposite arm. Stretch as far as you can and hold for 15 seconds. Repeat on both sides 10 times.

Leg Lifts

Lying on your back, lift one leg as far off the ground as possible. Hold for 15 seconds. Then relax and repeat, five times for each leg. Then, lift both legs off the ground at the same time and hold for 15 seconds. Relax and repeat five times.

Upper Body Lift

On your stomach, push your upper body up off the floor as far as possible, keeping your hips in contact with the floor at all times. Hold the position for 15 seconds and repeat five times.

Groin Stretch

Sit with your legs in front of you. Spread them in a V-shape as far apart as possible. Bend at the waist, leaning toward your left leg. Try to touch the bottom of your left foot with your

Single Leg Lifts
Raise one leg as high as possible. Hold for 15 seconds. Relax and repeat with the other leg.

hands. Hold the position for 15 seconds, then relax and stretch again. Repeat five times on both sides. Then relax and, bending at the waist, lean forward between your legs, trying to stretch forward so that your chest rests on the ground. Hold this position for 15 seconds, then relax and repeat five times.

As a variation, keep one leg extended, but pull the other leg in so that it is bent comfortably at the knee. Try to touch the foot of the extended leg with your hands. Hold this position for 10 seconds; repeat five times on each side.

Flexibility Exercises Throughout the Day

One of the best ways to improve flexibility is to perform flexibility exercises throughout the day. Instead of just setting aside 10 minutes a day of flexibility work, try to incorporate it into your daily schedule. For example, while you are at work, you can perform side bends or neck

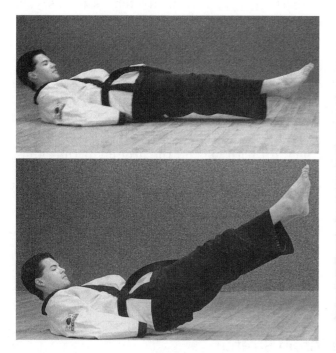

Double Leg Lifts
Raise both legs off the ground as far as possible. Hold for 15 seconds. Relax and repeat.

Upper Body Lift
Rest on your stomach. Push your upper body up off the floor, keeping your hips in contact with the floor. Hold for 15 seconds.

(1)

(2)

(3)

(4)

(5)

Groin Stretch

Sit with your legs apart as far as possible (1). Lean toward the left leg and hold for 15 seconds (2). Lean toward the right leg and hold for 15 seconds (3). Lean forward and hold for 15 seconds (4). Pull one leg in, bending the knee. Stretch toward the extended leg and hold for 15 seconds (5).

rotations while standing at your desk. In the morning, read the newspaper on the floor while doing a groin stretch. Perform leg lifts while watching your favorite television show. By adding these routines to your daily activities, you will gain much more flexibility than if you limit your exercises to a specific workout time. You may also find that these flexibility exercises will help relieve tension and stress.

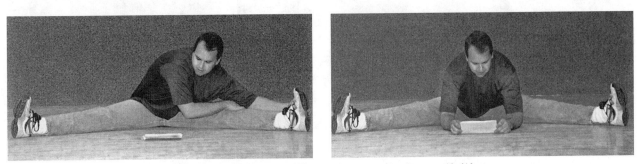

Perform stretches while doing everyday activities.

Flexibility Drills

Two different drills can help increase your flexibility while helping you improve your martial arts skills. The first one requires a partner, but the second can be done solo.

Kicking Drill

Work with a partner. If you have access to a focus mitt or other kicking target or pad, use it. Otherwise, have your partner use the palm of his hand as a target. Tell your partner which kicking techniques you have mastered. Begin in a fighting stance. Have your partner call out, at random, the kind of kick you are to perform.

At the same time, your partner should move the target to a low, middle, or high position. Moving quickly, perform the technique your partner has identified at the target height indicated. Stop only briefly between kicks.

Chambering Drill

To improve flexibility and ensure good tight chambers, stack cushions or pillows on the floor or a low bench and practice chambering your kick high enough to kick over the top of the cushions without knocking them over. Practice each of the kicks you know, adding cushions or pillows as your skill and flexibility increase.

Practice chambering kicks over target bags or cushions.

Increase the height of your stack to improve your chambering.

23

Speed Drills

The most important mathematical equation for martial artists is this: speed times mass equals power. For this reason, a small person can be as powerful as a large person, so long as the small person is very, very fast. Speed translates into power, and so it is an essential component of Tae Kwon Do training.

Speed Techniques

Certain Tae Kwon Do techniques require speed. The spinning wheel kicks is one of these. Speed alone makes the spinning wheel kick effective. If you aren't quick enough, this technique won't work, no matter how much muscle you put behind it. For such techniques, it is essential to acquire speed.

Speed Through Relaxation

Although it seems hard to believe, speed is best achieved through relaxation. The more relaxed you are, the quicker you can be. So the first thing you must do in Tae Kwon Do training is relax. To prove the point, try this: with your right arm chambered at your side, make a tight fist. Clench all the muscles in your arm so that you can see them working. Now punch forward as hard as you can. Next,

relax your arm muscles. Shake the tightness out. Make a loose fist, chambering your hand in a relaxed position near your waist. Now punch forward.

Makes a lot of difference, doesn't it? The second technique is much faster than the first. However, the second technique can become sloppy and less powerful if you're not careful. Therefore, you must tighten the muscle at the moment of impact. This is one reason why all Tae Kwon Do techniques emphasize the twist at the end. As you punch, for example, you will begin with your palm facing up. You arm should be relaxed. As your hand reaches the target, your wrist should twist so that your palm faces down. At the moment you begin the twist, you should tighten your muscles, clenching your fist for impact. This creates a quick and powerful technique.

Clench-and-Release

One way to practice muscle relaxation is the clench-and-release exercise. Starting with your arm, clench all of your muscles as tightly as possible and hold for about 15 seconds. Then, shake your arm loose, relaxing as much as you can. Repeat this process several times. Try it

217

on both arms and legs. Through this practice, you'll learn what a relaxed muscle feels like and can more readily relax before performing your techniques.

Snapping Movements

Adding a snapping or whipping movement to the end of each technique will increase the speed and force of your techniques. This is done simply by recoiling quickly. For example, if you punch and land your punch solidly, you will have a strong technique. However, the power of the punch will be only in the pushing motion that you have performed. You have eliminated the speed of the technique and so have reduced the power of it. On the other hand, if you punch and, after landing your punch, pull your punch back quickly, you'll be creating a snap at the end of your punch. This adds speed to your technique. The speed times the mass you have put behind the punch will increase the power considerably.

Try this: using a punching bag or target, punch as hard as you can, landing your punch solidly. Stop your punch when you reach your target. Then, punch as hard as you can, pulling your punch back to the starting position after it has reached the target, moving as quickly as you can. You should see a definite difference in speed and snap.

You can practice adding this snap or whip to the end of a technique by returning your hand or foot to its starting position (the chamber position) as soon as your strike has reached its target.

Plyometrics

One great way to improve jumping techniques is working on plyometric drills. These drills help you gain explosive power and explosive movements, which means improved agility and response time, too. The games you played as a kid are great for building plyometric speed — hopscotch, jump rope, and the like are all excellent ways of building speed.

Frog Jumps

Squat on the floor, keeping your hands out for balance. Leapfrog your way across the room as quickly as possible. Keep up continual leapfrogging for 30 seconds, adding on five seconds at a time. When you can do 60 leapfrogs in a minute, you'll have improved your speed considerably.

Frog Jumps
Crouch on the floor and leap into the air. Continue leaping for 30 seconds.

Jumping Drill
Jump from one side of a stack of targets or cushions to the other.

Jumping Drill

Stack cushions or pillows on the floor, starting with a height of about eight inches. Jump from one side of the stack to the other as quickly as you can without stopping and without knocking the cushions over. Stack the cushions higher as you improve. When you are able to stack the cushions as high as your knees and complete 15 jumps in 30 seconds, you'll have increased your speed considerably.

Sweeping Drill

Work with a partner for this drill. Have your partner use a blocking target (these are sold at martial arts supply houses). If a blocking target is not available, a long, flexible object will work — even the cardboard tube from a roll of wrapping paper can suffice. Have your partner sweep at your feet so that you must jump up to avoid hitting the target. Your partner should sweep back and forth quickly, without allowing pauses between jumps. Your partner can increase the height of the sweeps (aiming at the knees eventually) as you improve. Once you are able to jump as high as your knees and complete 20 jumps in 30 seconds, you'll have increased your speed considerably.

Sweeping Drill
Have your partner sweep at your feet. Jump to avoid being struck.

24

Strength Drills

Strength, of course, is the other element of power, and it requires equal dedication. Strength can be gained through a variety of means, including repetition of techniques and weight lifting. Keep in mind that as your strength and therefore muscle mass increases, your flexibility will decrease. It is important for a martial artist to keep the two in balance, so if you plan to work on building strength, you will need to perform additional flexibility exercises.

Weight Lifting

Although many martial artists do start lifting weights to increase their strength, it isn't necessary. If you have access to a weight room, or choose to purchase free weights (these can be found fairly inexpensively at sporting goods stores), certain lifts are more valuable for the martial artist than others. These include the military press, the lateral pull-down, lateral raise, squat/leg press, hamstring curl, leg extensions, chest press, biceps curl, and triceps extension. Add the hip adductor/abductor, and you're set.

Isometric/Isotonic Exercises

Exercises that require you to lift your own body weight are excellent for building strength. These include crunches, pull-ups, and push-ups. And since they require little or no equipment, they're very cost-effective.

Crunches
Lie on the floor, knees bent, feet on the floor (left). Curl shoulders and upper body forward off the floor.

Crunches

Crunches work your abdominal muscles. Although sit-ups were once recommended for strengthening this area of the body, they are now considered too dangerous.

Lie on the floor, knees slightly bent, feet on the floor. Put your hands behind your ears. Don't put your hands under your neck or lace your fingers together; this creates too much strain on your neck. Using your abdominal muscles, roll forward so that your shoulders lift off the ground. Moving slowly and deliberately, return to your starting position. You need to move slowly and smoothly to avoid using momentum instead of muscles to do the work. Repeat the crunch 15 times.

Here are some variations you can use:

■ Twist to the right, as shown below, as you crunch by leading with your left shoulder. Then twist to the left by leading with your right shoulder. This type of crunch works your oblique abdominal muscles which are otherwise hard to tone.

■ Extend your legs and lift them in the air 45 degrees, then 90 degrees as you perform each crunch.

Lift legs 45 degrees into the air while performing crunches (above), then lift them 90 degrees into the air (right).

Boxer Sit-Ups

Work with a partner. Lie on your back, head slightly between the feet of your partner, who should be standing. Grasp your partner's ankles and raise your legs 90 degrees. Have your partner push your legs down forcefully. Don't let them touch the ground. Lift your legs back up and have your partner push them down again. Work as quickly as possible. Repeat 15 times.

As a variation, have your partner push your legs to the right or the left instead of straight down.

Push-Ups

Lie flat on the floor and place your palms on the floor directly under your shoulders, about shoulders' width apart. Keeping your abdomen tight and your back and shoulders straight, push up. Rest your knees on the floor if necessary. Repeat 15 times. Add push-ups in increments of five as you improve, until you can do 75 resting only your palms and toes on the floor.

Variations work different muscle groups. These are done by changing the placement of your hands. Spread your hands so they are extended two shoulders' widths apart to work your shoulder muscles. Bring your hands in close under your sternum to work your triceps. Finally, work on the knuckle push-up. These are done by making your hands into fists and resting your weight on the first two knuckles of each hand (your punching knuckles). Knuckle push-ups strengthen your wrists so that they won't roll when you punch.

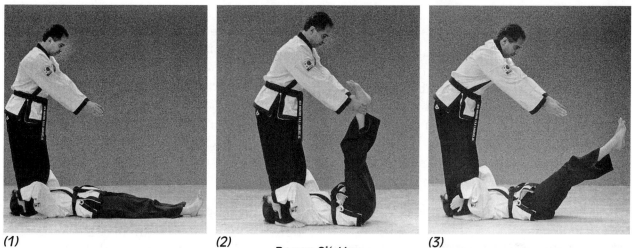

(1) *(2)* *(3)*

Boxer Sit-Ups

Work with a partner. With your partner standing, lie on your back, head between your partner's legs. Grasp your partner's ankles (1). Raise your legs until your partner can reach them (2). Your partner should throw your legs toward the ground and you should keep your legs from touching the ground (3). Lift your legs and repeat.

(1)

(2)

(3)

(4)

(5) ### Push-Ups
Lie on the floor with your palms directly under the shoulders (1). Push straight up (2). As a variation, spread the arms wider (3). In another variation, bring the hands in under your sternum (4). An old martial arts standby is the knuckle push-up (5).

Pull-Ups

If a pull-up bar (sometimes called a chin-up) is available, work on pull-ups. If you can't do these well at first, have a partner act as spotter. Grip the bar with hands about shoulders' width apart and pull straight up. Your goal should be to perform 15 or more without a spotter's help.

Variations work different muscle groups. These can be done by changing your grip on the bar. You can widen your grip or use a backward grip.

Building Strength Through Martial Arts Techniques

Practicing kicks and punches full power is one way to increase strength. You'll need a heavy bag to do this, or a strong partner with a kicking target. Your goal should be to knock the heavy bag (or your partner) back at least several inches with every technique. Practice techniques in a continual motion for two-minute rounds for the best workout.

If you don't have access to a heavy bag or a cooperative partner, you can still build strength through practicing martial arts techniques by slow-motion kicking. This is actually a great drill even if you do have a partner and a heavy bag.

Begin by practicing your techniques slowly in front of a mirror. Although you can practice hand techniques in slow motion, the real strength building comes when you practice kicks slowly. Use this time to perfect your techniques, as well. Look at your chamber. Is it high? Is it tight? Is your foot in the correct position? Is your body straight? As you get the hang of kicking slowly (it requires balance and a certain amount of practice), continually slow down your kicks until it looks as if you are practicing in slow motion. Gradually increase the amount of time it takes for you to do each kick. Aim for a goal of spending an entire 60 seconds on one technique. Practice each of your kicks on each of your legs 10 times for an excellent strength building workout.

Conclusion

With dedication and practice, you can become a highly skilled practitioner of Tae Kwon Do. By practicing Tae Kwon Do at least three days a week, you'll be the equivalent of a brown belt in a year. By then, you'll be able to move on to more advanced techniques. Even so, the basic and intermediate techniques shown here take literally a lifetime to master, as there is always a way to do a technique more perfectly.

Tae Kwon Do practice will make you stronger and more confident in many ways, able to meet the challenges of the training hall and the world outside it. Although the keys to Tae Kwon Do include physical skills, such as developing strength and speed, mental skills, such as working with confidence, should not be regarded lightly. Further, emotional skills, such as those outlined in the Five Tenets, are essential to a deeper understanding of Tae Kwon Do. Only by living with courtesy, integrity, perseverance, self-control, and indomitable spirit will a fighter become a true martial artist.

The study of Tae Kwon Do goes beyond mere self-defense. The true secret of Tae Kwon Do lies inside, for as you practice, you will seek self-understanding and enlightenment. You have already started on the path. Good luck on the way.

Sample Workout

Warming up and Stretching — 5 minutes

Techniques Practice — 15 minutes
      Hand Techniques and Stances
      Blocking
      Kicking Techniques
      Elbow and Knee Striking Techniques

Takedown Techniques and Step Sparring — 5 minutes

Freestyle Sparring — 10 minutes
      Footwork
      Timing Technique Drills
      Combination Drills

Self-Defense Techniques — 10 minutes

Chon-ji Form — 5 minutes
Cooling down — 5 minutes

Optional
      Meditation
      Breathing Techniques

Workouts should be fun.

Glossary

AP CHAKI — a front kick.

AP HURYA CHAKI — a hooking kick.

BAL OHMKIGI — footwork or stepping techniques.

BANGO — all blocking or evasive techniques.

BARO — a command meaning "finish."

BO DAE RYUN — step sparring.

CHAKI — any kicking technique. Also spelled *chagi*.

CHANG KWON CHIGI — a palm strike.

CHAREYHET — a command meaning "attention."

CHI — inner energy or life force that can be summoned to give extra energy when needed. *Chi* is also thought to help the martial artist focus and concentrate in order to succeed.

CHIKI CHAKI — a crescent kick.

CHIREU-GI — a straight punch, sometimes called a "corkscrew punch," since the wrist twists at the end of the technique.

CHONGUL JA SAE — a front stance.

CHOOMUK DUNG CHIGI — a backfist strike.

CHOOMUK-PAHDAK CHIGI — a hammer fist strike.

CHU GYO NIM — a Tae Kwon Do instructor with a black belt rank below fourth dan.

CHUNBEE — a command meaning "ready."

CHUNG KWON CHIGI — a straight punch.

CHUNYE — see KYUNG YEH.

DALYEUN-JU — a striking post used to toughen the knuckles and condition hands for punching and striking.

DO — in martial arts, a term meaning "the way." This is a concept that suggests that martial arts are not just sports or methods of self-defense, but are in fact ways of life.

DOBOK — the traditional Tae Kwon Do uniform consisting of loose, baggy pants and a jacket that closes at the waist with a belt indicating the wearer's rank.

DOHRAS (or DERO DOHRAS) — a command meaning "turn around," usually given to instruct a student to adjust his or her uniform, especially after physical exertion may have caused it to loosen. Tae Kwon Do students always turn away (therefore, "turn around") from the front of the *dojang* and the instructor to attend to such matters, as a sign of courtesy.

DOJANG — a Tae Kwon Do training hall.

DOLL RYE CHAKI (or DEUL RYE CHAKI) — a roundhouse kick.

DOLL RYE MAKI — a spear block.

DTUIYU — a word meaning "flying," applied to kicking techniques. A *dtuiyu yup chaki* is a flying side kick.

DWET CHAKI — a reverse kick.

EIDAN (or EIDAN CHAKI) — a jumping technique, especially a jump kick.

GOMAN — a command meaning to finish and return to the starting position.

HADAN — a word meaning "low." It applies to techniques and their target area. For instance, a *hadan ap chaki* is a front kick to the opponent's knee or ankle.

HOGU — sparring gear, protective equipment such as foot and hand coverings used to prevent injury during sparring.

HUGUL JA SAE — a back stance.

HYUNG — a word for "form."

JA YU DAE RYUN — free sparring.

JUNGDAN — a word meaning "middle." It applies to techniques and their target area. For example, a *jungdan ap chaki* is a front kick to the opponent's midsection.

JUNGDAN MAKI — a crescent block.

KAMSANEDAH — a Korean word meaning "thank you."

KIHOP — the expression of chi, such as is needed for focus and concentration. The name for the yell or shout that martial artists use when sparring, board breaking, or performing techniques that require special energy and attention.

KIM JA SAE — a horse stance.

KONG KEOK — a straight punch.

KUK-KI-WON — the international headquarters of Korean martial arts. Located in Seoul, the building was constructed in 1973, and houses the World Tae Kwon Do Federation governing body. Its primary purpose is to unify the different styles of Tae Kwon Do. Training, examinations and teaching certification are offered.

KWAN — a Korean word for school, as in a *Tae Kwon Do kwan*.

KWAN JANG — the head instructor of a school.

KWANSU — a spear hand technique

KYUNG YEH — a command meaning "bow." It is used to instruct two (or more) Tae Kwon Do students to bow to each other to show respect and courtesy.

MAKI — a blocking technique.

MOOHRUP CHAKI — a knee striking technique.

NOTCHWOH SAE — an exaggerated front stance, usually used to build leg muscle strength.

PAHL-KOOM-CHI CHIGI — an elbow striking technique.

PAHL MAKI — a forearm block.

PAHN CHUN JA SAE — a short front stance that can be used in sparring.

PILSUNG — a Korean word meaning "certain victory," used whenever two Tae Kwon Do practitioners work together, to express appreciation.

POOMSE — a Korean word meaning "form."

SA BEUM NIM — a Tae Kwon Do instructor with a black belt rank at or above the fourth dan.

SANGDAN — a Korean word meaning "high." It applies to techniques and their target area. For example, a *sangdan ap chaki* is a front kick to the opponent's head.

SIJAK — a command meaning "begin."

SUDO — a knife hand technique.

UM YANG — the Korean term for *yin-yang*. See YIN-YANG.

YANG PAHL MAKI — a double forearm block.

YEOP SUDO — a ridge hand technique.

YIN-YANG — the concept, fundamental to Tae Kwon Do practice, that life is made up of conflicting but harmonious elements, such as night and day. One does not exist without the other. Yin-yang is used in Tae Kwon Do to understand the need for balance between the mental, physical and emotional aspects of the art. Maintaining balance and moderation in all things is essential to a productive and rewarding life.

YUP CHAKI — a side kick.

YUP SAE — a side stance, like the T-stance.

Black Belt Degrees

ILDAN — First Dan (Degree) Black Belt
EADAN — Second Dan
SAMDAN — Third Dan
SIADAN — Fourth Dan
OHDAN — Fifth Dan
YUKDAN — Sixth Dan
CHILDAN — Seventh Dan
PALDAN — Eighth Dan
KUDAN — Ninth Dan

Korean Numbers

HANA — one
DEUL — two
SET — three
NET — four
DASET — five
YUHSET — six
ILGOP — seven
YEOLDEOL — eight
AHOP — nine
YEOL — ten
YEOLHANA — eleven
YEOLDEUL — twelve
YEOLSET — thirteen
YEOLNET — fourteen
YEOLDASET — fifteen
YEOLYUHSET — sixteen
YEOLILGOP — seventeen
YEOLYEOLDEOL — eighteen
YEOLAHOP — nineteen
SOOMUL — twenty
SERUN — thirty
MAHRON — forty
OSIP — fifty
BEK — one hundred